Studying Childhood and Early Childhood

A GUIDE FOR STUDENTS

1412907462

Studying Childhood and Early Childhood

A GUIDE FOR STUDENTS

Kay Sambell, Sue Miller
and Mel Gibson

P·C·P

Paul Chapman
Publishing

Paul Chapman Publishing
A SAGE Publications Company
1 Oliver's Yard
55 City Road
London EC1Y 1SP

SAGE Publications Inc
2455 Teller Road
Thousand Oaks, California 91320

SAGE Publications India Pvt Ltd
B-42, Panchsheel Enclave
Post Box 4109
New Delhi 110 017

Library of Congress Control Number: 2004117795

A catalogue record for this book is available from the British Library

ISBN 1–4129-0745–4
ISBN 1–4129-0746–2 (pbk)

Typeset by Dorwyn Ltd, Wells, Somerset
Printed in Great Britain by T.J. International, Padstow, Cornwall

Contents

About the Authors

Professor Kay Sambell has led Northumbria University's BA Joint Honours degree in Childhood Studies for a number of years. Since gaining her PhD in 1996 for a thesis entitled 'The Use of Future Fictional Time in Novels for Young Readers', Kay has been involved in a wide range of research and development activities. Some have focused on her own discipline area, Childhood Studies and Children's Literature, while others have involved working across a range of disciplines, focusing on developing alternative formative assessment strategies within core teaching in order to better support the learning approaches of diverse student groups. She has published widely, especially on the topic of students' perspectives of innovative assessment, and has presented her work to a range of national and international audiences.

In 2002 Kay was awarded a National Teaching Fellowship by the Higher Education Funding Council for her work on assessment. She has collaborated with a number of other UK National Teaching Fellows to further develop diverse strategies to enhance autonomous learning via assessment and is currently co-directing a large-scale Fund for the Development of Teaching & Learning (FDTL5) project which aims to improve learning and teaching in Childhood Studies through a focus on academic literacy. She has a lead role in Northumbria University's Centre for Excellence in Assessment for Learning. In September 2004 Kay was awarded a Personal Chair in Learning and Teaching, Childhood Studies, becoming Northumbria University's first 'Teaching Professor'.

Sue Miller works for Newcastle City Council where she has the strategic lead for the development of the City's Sure Start and Children's Centres programme and is also the Lead Officer for the Early Years Development and Childcare Partnership. Prior to this she was a Senior Lecturer at Northumbria University where she helped to develop and then went on to run the BA Joint Honours degree Care and Education (Early Years).

Sue has worked for more than twenty years in local authorities in the North East where she has been a teacher, senior educational psychologist and senior manager in Children's Services. She speaks and publishes widely on the challenges of reshaping services for families and young children and working across professional disciplines. She is probably best known for her publications in parenting education: *Positive Parenting* and *Let's Talk Parenting*, which are widely used by parents and practitioners within the private, voluntary and maintained sectors both in this country and abroad.

Dr Mel Gibson lectures on the BA Honours degree in Childhood Studies at Northumbria University. She has, in collaboration with Kay Sambell, won a number of teaching and learning awards for her innovative work on bringing the 'real world' into the classroom via 'virtual visiting'. She specializes in young people and media. Mel's doctoral thesis was on British women's memories of reading comics as girls and she has published widely in this area.

She is also a consultant running training and promotional events about visual literacy in picture books, comics and other media. Mel has regularly advised libraries, schools and other organizations since 1993, when she was a key contributor to *Graphic Account*, a book published by the Youth Libraries Group dedicated to the subject of developing graphic novels collections for 16- to 25-year-olds.

Acknowledgements

With special thanks to our students and graduates, especially:

Sara Bishop, Catherine Coatsworth, Eleanor Havery, Suzanne Powell, Helen Smith, Helen Waistall and Gillian Whinnam, who have acted as superb 'critical friends'.

Our thanks, too, go to the Northumbria Childhood course teaching teams and others who have supported the development of the teaching experience on offer to our students, including Professor Maria Filomena Gaspar, Denise Keighley, Judith Kernen and Nigel Stinton.

Finally, thanks to our families, and to Jude Bowen, Charlotte Saunders and all at SAGE, for their support during the development of this book.

Preface

This book is designed to provide students studying Childhood Studies (CS) and Early Childhood Studies (ECS) in higher education with the means to do better, to be more successful and to work towards achieving the learning outcomes of such courses with greater confidence and insight. We decided to write this book because, having taught on a range of CS/ECS courses since the early 1990s, we realized that today's student of childhood all too often faces a number of challenges in degree-level study, challenges that are related to the newness of this exciting, but potentially bewildering, field of enquiry.

Having worked closely with hundreds of students, we felt that we were familiar with the sorts of problems, worries and misunderstandings that crop up for a large proportion of learners, and that we have developed an understanding of the sorts of advice and guidance that will overcome these worries and so enable students to make the most of their time at university. We came to feel that students coming onto the increasing number of CS/ECS courses springing up in universities could benefit from our collective hindsight and that this was the time to draw all our experiences together. In this book, then, you will learn about CS/ECS courses from people who have 'been there, done that and got the t-shirt'. These people include students who have undertaken such courses, as well as their lecturers, assessors and future employers.

The book is full of students' voices, case studies and worked examples. We favoured this approach because our students have told us how useful it is for them to hear from peers as well as lecturers. In fact, one of the most useful things you can do is to go and talk about your studies with 'old hands' – students from the year above you, or those who have graduated, because this 'insider information' helps you get to grips with what you can and should do if you want to do well. That's what this book is all about.

WHO WILL FIND OUR BOOK USEFUL?

Our book is aimed specifically at undergraduates who are just setting out on CS or ECS degree courses at university. Again, personal experience tells us that these courses tend to attract a wide variety of students, all of whom have different needs and who bring vastly different prior experiences of study to university.

Of those students some will have fairly 'traditional' entry qualifications, such as 'A' levels, although they can range from subjects where essay writing is central, such as History and English, through to Maths and Science. Many students are likely to have other entry qualifications, such as HNCs, CACHE Diplomas (Nursery Nurse), BTEC National Awards or Certificates, and HEFC Access Certificates.

A number of students will have come straight from school or college. For others, it may well be a long time since they last studied academically, as these subject areas also attract many mature students seeking to return to education.

In addition, it is certainly the case that an increasing number of students will be the first in their family to go to university, and so may be very unsure about what to expect. Going to university is a huge transition and it can make people feel insecure, wondering if they belong on degree-level courses, or if they'll make the grade, especially at the start of their degree, and particularly if studying is unfamiliar, or they have a specific learning difficulty such as dyslexia. This book is designed to help all students get to grips with their degrees, to help build confidence, so that every one of you makes the transition to studying childhood at university level smoothly and quickly.

The richness of this mixture of student experience and background highlights the fact that there isn't a single 'model' student of childhood. In the same way that no two CS or ECS courses will look quite the same, each having a different slant according to lecturers' research interests, for instance, so no two students will have the same lifestyles or domestic circumstances.

One thing that many students do have in common, however, is that they are under pressure, and have other commitments, including work. For instance, CS and ECS are female-dominated subject areas, which is likely to mean that many of the students on your course will combine their studies with being the primary carer within a household.

Most students will also need to look for paid employment while they study. However, CS/ECS students are well placed to make a virtue of such necessity. Indeed, we would argue that if you eventually want to work with or for children, young people, their families or relevant agencies it is useful to undertake voluntary activities and employment beyond the course in areas that relate to childhood. The later chapters of our book will help you think, sooner rather than later, about finding work that helps you build up a set of experiences and contacts. Even better, choosing your work carefully will allow you to weave your working life into the fabric of your study in, say, dissertation or project work. In doing so, you place yourself in front of the competition when it comes to getting a job after university.

Chapter 1

How to Use This Book

HOW TO USE THE CHAPTERS

The chapter you are reading now is designed to be a 'route finder' through the book's content, explaining what it is for, how it should be used and what it can and can't do for you. We think you'll benefit most if you go through the chapters from start to finish, rather than just dipping into the book. Chapters 2, 3 and 4 are all designed to help you approach your assignments productively, by focusing on the various interrelated processes and stages of learning about childhood. Although we have, for ease of reading, teased them out into three different 'phases' – making the most of lectures, tackling academic reading and producing a good assignment – they are, in fact, all interwoven.

These chapters are full of examples and illustrative material drawn from real courses, but you need to use these alongside the actual material being studied on your particular course. The idea is that the examples will help you to understand your own tutors' expectations, and help you to develop strategies for tackling their demands. In coming to understand the key themes, issues and questions posed on your specific course, you will improve how you approach learning, and do better in your assignments.

The final two chapters focus attention on what you might want to do after your degree finishes. Thinking ahead can help you make good choices when it comes to, say, selecting topics for an independent study or picking research observation visits, so reading the final chapters at the outset of your course will help you ensure that you don't close any doors for yourself when it comes to getting your dream job. Chapter 5 sets out practical guidance which is designed to help take you through the process of applying for and getting jobs, and you will probably want to refer to most of it in your final year when formal applications need, generally, to be in. Three years seems a long time at the start of a course, but it flies by, and former graduates, from whom you'll hear in the final chapter, repeatedly say they wished they had started thinking about possible opportunities and using their degree and vacation work to build up relevant experience a lot earlier than they did. This is your chance to learn from their experience! You'll get some practical ideas for things you can put into action, from places to start looking for work to ways of presenting what you have learned on your course. These ideas will partly come from hearing what previous students are doing now, what it entails, and how they got to where they wanted to be.

To summarize, then, this book should help you make the most of your time at university by helping you see the point of the degree you are studying and identifying what tutors are aiming to do in creating the courses they have. It will also help you learn from others' experiences (and mistakes). The book provides you with a set of questions to ask yourself about the degree and what you want to get out of it. These will help you 'tune in' to CS and ECS, in terms of key themes and issues, effective study patterns, achieving your best in assessment, using your course to build up your curriculum vitae, and selling yourself well in the jobs market.

WHY IS THERE A NEED FOR OUR STUDENT GUIDE TO STUDYING CS/ECS?

You might be wondering why we don't just outline the content of CS/ECS courses and provide you with a summary of the major points and information you need to know to pass well. One thing is that CS/ECS, like all degrees, just cannot be simplified in that way. In addition, since the mid-1990s, a huge number of courses have sprung up in this area, all of which are quite different in flavour or essence, as we mention above. It's a very exciting time, as public attention and national policy have focused on children and childhood at a range of levels in recent years. In turn this has had, and will continue to have, an impact

- on the sorts of jobs that are available

- on the kinds of professionals who are needed

- on the sorts of courses universities make available.

Furthermore, academically speaking, CS/ECS is, itself, in its infancy, and as a subject is undergoing rapid evolution and change. CS/ECS is quickly becoming recognized as a 'new' subject area or academic field of enquiry in its own right, and a rich, complex and hugely diverse one. As a consequence, this can make it hard to get to grips with the expectations of your specific course and those who teach on it.

Traditionally matters relating to children and childhood have been taught in universities as an aspect of several disciplines, all of which have tended to use different ways of studying children, using different methods and drawing on different ideas and principles. Some, such as education or psychology, have concentrated on the child, children or young people. Others, such as sociology or cultural studies, have concentrated on childhood as an idea or concept. Your course may actually be basically rooted in these sorts of approaches. But increasingly some of the courses developing in CS/ECS now question their own identity and approach, as literature is rapidly emerging that tries to straddle these divisions between disciplines and transform it into a 'new' academic field. This field is interdisciplinary, which means that it consciously draws on the different perspectives offered by, say, sociology, social history and psychology to think about exciting new ways of understanding children and childhood.

Many of the courses springing up are along these lines. They focus on new ways of looking at children and childhood and explore new, more integrated ways of theorizing childhood. When national policy (as we mentioned earlier) places the child at the centre it redefines the ways in which professionals work with and relate to that theoretical child. New policy initiatives, such as the setting up of Children's Centres and the integration of children's services, demand a workforce that can think critically and analytically, creatively and sensitively about childhood, a workforce that can 'think outside the box'. Such ways of thinking value open-mindedness over dogma and innovation over doing things the way in which they have always been done. Many courses, such as the one headed up for a number of years by one of the authors, Sue Miller, set out quite deliberately to prepare students to acquire the skills, knowledge and values of multi-professional Early Years agencies and settings. On that course the students are taught by tutors from a range of professions in the areas of Health, Education and Social Work. Other courses, like the one headed up by Kay Sambell and Mel Gibson at Northumbria University, encourage students to explore different disciplinary approaches to the study of childhood, by engaging with topics as varied as children's comics and books, school governance, historical archive material, parenting, social policy and representations of childhood. Students are taught by academics that include historians, literature specialists, cultural studies tutors and geographers.

We draw your attention to the rich diversity of courses that go under the general name of CS/ECS right from the start, because, to do well, you must learn to identify the specific approach your own course takes and the local context of your own course. Our book, therefore, sets out to give you a helping hand by encouraging you to think carefully about the key dimensions of your course and offers some handy hints which should get you off to a flying start rather than meaning that you have to pick up important information slowly and painfully through trial and error. Whatever you do, don't assume that all courses are the same. Thinking carefully about your course and its particular outlook, aims and objectives will enable you to understand its specific expectations sooner rather than later, allowing you to make the most of your studies, make sense of your prior and personal experiences (which all courses will value and seek to build upon) and achieve your potential. That's why we think you should try to use our book early in your course, so that you tune into what it is trying to encourage you to know and do.

We believe that thinking carefully about your course as a whole, and even on a module-by-module level, is a fundamental aspect of success on CS/ECS programmes. In our experience students are often surprised by the particular demands of courses, especially if they were expecting CS/ECS courses to be very like the more practically or vocationally oriented courses they had studied prior to coming to university, such as NNEB courses. No matter what appears in publicity material and at open days, some students arrive at university expecting their course to consist entirely of hands-on experience with children. They tell us they never expected, say, to be studying history, and this means they feel quite lacking in confidence and even motivation, until they grasp the point of why historical approaches to childhood are an important aspect of their study. That courses are often rather more academic than practice based means that some students are surprised to find that, far from being an easier option, CS/ECS courses demand students to read widely and work energetically on their research and essay-writing skills to achieve good results.

When there is a mismatch like this, there is a huge gap between lecturers' understandings and students' assumptions about what it means to study childhood at university. This means that everyone has to work hard to minimize that gap if all students are to enjoy their studies and be successful. That's precisely what this book sets out to help you do, so that you can make the most of the course on which you have enrolled. It does this through helping you understand what you are expected to do, and offering tips and strategies for undertaking the work.

HOW CAN YOU TELL WHAT YOUR COURSE'S APPROACH IS?

Where is it located?

The first thing to do is to identify where your course is taught within the structure of academic disciplines of your university. Broadly speaking, CS/ECS is usually taught under the umbrella of Social Sciences and Humanities, but you can learn a lot by getting a closer focus on it than this.

One way of sorting this out in your own mind is by looking at which School, Department or Faculty your course sits in. For example, is it in Education, Health, Cultural Studies or Social Studies? Is it offered in just one department, or a few? Getting answers to all these questions can tell you a lot about the sort of emphasis it is likely to have.

Who teaches on the course and what are their particular research interests?

What a lecturer's discipline and research interests are is not always apparent to a student, but it is important because each discipline has its own academic outlooks and perspectives, and this has an impact on what is taught and so on what you need to know to do well. So, for instance, the people who teach you may view themselves as primarily an

English specialist, a historian, an anthropologist, a psychologist and so on and that will influence the course. On the other hand, your course may be taught mainly by child-professionals (such as qualified teachers, health visitors, playworkers, social workers) who will base their teaching on those professional perspectives. Finally, the course might quite consciously set out to offer you a mix of professional and academic perspectives on the child. We give you particular advice in Chapter 2 on how to identify your lecturers' perspectives, by looking carefully at the words they use to describe the study of childhood and finding out what terms they find problematic or even offensive. You can start, though, by looking up their publications, either through an online bookshop like Amazon, or, even more usefully, by looking at the university website, which should offer both biographies and bibliographies of the staff teaching on your course. What they write and what their professional background is should help you to find out whether their CS/ECS teaching is the main aspect of their job, or if they teach on other, more mainstream, courses.

What approach does your course take as a whole?

Many of the people who work on CS/ECS courses would class their work as interdisciplinary – indeed, this is becoming increasingly common. Again, confusingly they don't all mean the same thing by 'interdisciplinarity'. Sometimes they mean you get to study childhood from different academic disciplinary perspectives, sometimes they try to meld this into a holistic approach. Some courses concentrate on the many diverse ways childhood is viewed with regard to time, place, age, ethnicity and other variables. CS/ECS can also be informed by a critique of the ways in which children's lives are governed and regulated, dominated by adults. Courses may also be underpinned by an emphasis on children as participants in society and decision-makers – and consequently have a child-centred approach or children's rights as a dominant theme. Asking yourself, 'where does my lecturer stand in relation to this?' or, 'do all my lecturers agree, or do they have quite different viewpoints?' will help you to sort this out and Chapter 2 will guide you through. In asking these questions you will start to develop a reflective approach to your course.

You and course themes

Generally speaking, the new student of childhood must learn to take a *thematic* approach to study. Figure 1.1 illustrates the complexity of this way of studying: childhood is the theme at the core of your study, but there are lots of different ways of approaching that theme.

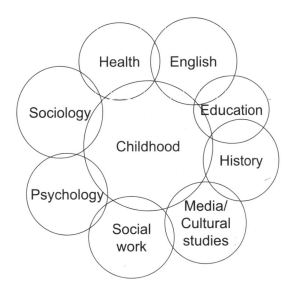

Figure 1.1 A thematic approach to studying Childhood and Early Childhood Studies

Students on CS/ECS courses are encouraged to simultaneously engage with a range of interlinked disciplinary perspectives, which means they might be expected to draw on recent research and theories including sociology, psychology, cultural studies, social history, philosophy, social policy and children's rights. In practice, this means that students have to 'know their way around' a whole host of disciplines and be able to use the different patterns and ways of constructing and talking about knowledge that they contain. As you read across a number of disciplines you will discover an extensive lexicon of terminology, approaches and conventions, in what can be described as a 'joined up' approach to study.

In very practical terms, the thematic approach means you have to learn to navigate round areas of the library as diverse as Sociology, Social Policy, Education, Women's Studies, Cultural and Media Studies,

Literature and Social History. Although each of these areas overlaps, as your course shows, they often use different terms to describe childhood and the issues around it. Chapter 3, 'Reading Into Writing', guides you through the tricky process of managing the different languages used by different academic cultures, which you need to learn to use in your writing if you wish to do well.

The difference from vocational courses

Whichever the prevalent nature of your course, there is no doubt that you will be expected to study different *perspectives* on childhood, explore themes of change and context, respond to questions and take part in debates. The various agendas surrounding childhood and children's lives are shifting: in the law, in social policy and in calls for integrated approaches to the care and education of young children in the UK. The way that CS/ECS courses engage with these agendas is what makes them distinct from those training students to be professional childcare workers such as teachers, nursery nurses or children's nurses.

This book helps you to get to grips with CS/ECS as academic courses, where you'll spend most of your time in a library or lecture room, rather than being out applying and putting into practice skills that you need to have in a professional role. This does not mean that CS/ECS courses are irrelevant to the real lives of children – far from it, as the students' comments in later chapters indicate – but it is important that you grasp the precise rationale for studying childhood in theory, as understanding this will stand you in good stead both during the course and later in the employment market.

You and learning at university – getting to grips with independent learning about childhood

This book offers insights into how best to become an effective independent learner, something that will become increasingly important as you move through your degree. Courses change as you progress from first to final year, with later years offering you more opportunities to work independently and with less direction from lecturers. This book will help by focusing upon the key learning processes that relate to the study of children's and young people's lives. It will outline effective, and ineffective, ways of going about study, giving you ideas for what to do and things to definitely avoid.

Throughout the book we hope to encourage you to think about the sort of learner you are and the kind of learning you enjoy, and how to develop appropriate study skills that are relevant to CS/ECS. To do this we emphasize the *process* rather than specific content or subject matter. The book works as a 'how to' guide, by getting you to explore the themes, issues, recurrent questions and approaches contained within your course. Use this book alongside the material you study on your course, and the specific recommended reading.

In particular, Chapter 2 will help you understand what academic skills and qualities CS/ECS courses seek to develop in their students, and how lecturers try to facilitate that. It will introduce common key themes and issues and enable you to unpack the way that, by taking childhood as a legitimate area for study, they provide opportunities for students to 'see' that there is a wide range of different views and perspectives about what childhood is for and to 'wake up' to these differences. It will explain that the starting point for understanding another's perspective is firstly to recognize your own, and that therefore personal responses and writing can be useful ways of beginning to see, reflect on and understand childhood.

It also explains that whatever the specific content or subject matter, most courses will want you, fundamentally, to *think*, *question*, enquire and interrogate. It will enable you to identify the key questions that lecturers want you to get to grips with on *your* course, help you to understand, on the most immediate level, what is meant by 'theory' and what common methods and activities tutors will use.

Chapter 3 then concentrates on reading, and gives worked examples of effective (and ineffective) approaches to reading, finding and using information about childhood. To do well at university, especially in Social Sciences and Humanities, which tend to be writing-intensive courses, you have to be able to become fluent in the appropriate ways of talking and writing about relevant ideas and concepts in relation to your subject. The best way to do this is via talking and rehearsing ideas and practising, *before* it 'counts' in a piece of work that is going to be assessed. Talking and reading about the main themes, issues and ideas in seminars with fellow students are the first steps to writing effectively and getting good marks.

Chapter 4 does the same for writing and presenting your ideas formally, for assessment. In our experience, those students who do well are able to see that writing at university requires them to make a transition, and they invest a lot of thought and energy in making sure they are clear about the differences between their approaches to writing before university, and how to write on their courses. After all, another aspect of doing well is tuning in to how you are going to be expected to learn and to be assessed. This chapter gets you to think about your approaches to assessment (building on earlier chapters) and allows you to hear from successful and less successful students, so that you can get the best marks you can.

The final chapters ask you to look ahead, during your course, to getting a job and to life after university, and help you to think and plan your studies so that you build up a body of evidence, knowledge and experience that you can capitalize on and use to help sell your skills in the workplace. They will show you how to make the most of the experiences you have to date, equipping you to get the most out of the degree by building on what you already know and are interested in. These chapters will also encourage you to consider, in time to do something about it, whether there are other experiences you have had or knowledge you have acquired (for example, through taking a gap year, through work experience, or through reading) that might help you to hit the ground running while on your course and, importantly, after it finishes.

Chapter 2

Key Course Themes

This chapter is designed to help you to make the move to the university-level study of childhood as smoothly and swiftly as possible.

KNOWING WHAT TO EXPECT

CS/ECS courses usually attract people with a wide range of prior experiences, and so students are likely to have an equally wide spectrum of feelings about studying childhood at degree level. Some lack confidence because it seems that many of their peers have previously taken child-focused courses, while they have not. Others may initially feel that they're being asked to cover old ground and that they know the subject well already.

This chapter shows that no matter what you have done before coming to university, *everyone* has something new to learn, adjustments to make and study skills to develop. No matter how much, or how little, prior experience of studying childhood or working with children you have, you will usually need to adjust your thinking, and your approaches to study so that you can contribute and draw from the new learning opportunities university study affords. Indeed, you may well hear lecturers say that they are still learning about childhood themselves, because the sort of learning you do at university is never 'done' – there are always new insights to be gained and connections to be made.

It's worth remembering, too, that *everyone* has valuable experiences to offer. We hope by the end of this chapter you will see how much you have to gain from developing good working relationships with your fellow students, as well as your lecturers.

PROBLEMATIZING CHILDHOOD

Making the move to studying childhood at university basically involves seeing childhood in new, increasingly complicated ways. Most courses will encourage you to identify and take stock of what you already know about children and childhood, whether that is theoretical knowledge or the practical work of bringing up children, or your own experience of being a child. Your lecturers, though, are likely to move you gradually away from personal to more theorized views of children and their lives, encouraging you to see childhood as a complex, problematic concept, rather than a straightforward, natural phase that we all go through. This chapter highlights some of the ways they might encourage you to see childhood afresh, waking up to 'taken-for-granted' notions about children and childhood.

In short, your lecturers are looking for *far* more than common-sense ideas, or a set of facts about children's development: they eventually want you to be able to analyse children's lives and environments; the products and policies that are made for them; their experiences and the views of professionals who work with and for them. In a nutshell, they will want you to be able to analyse ideas and meanings associated with 'the child' and 'childhood' and see that talking about childhood is actually a very demanding thing to do. They hope that during your time at university you will get deeply involved in exploring, discussing and debating a range of varying ideas and perspectives on the meanings of childhood.

The words lecturers might use to describe this process include

As an idea childhood is	Discussing it is
● Contested	● Intricate
● Problematical	● Complicated
● Complex	● Involved
● Debatable	● Discursive
● Challenging	● About perceiving key questions, rather than seeking answers or final solutions to problems

THE IMPLICATIONS: THERE'S NO 'CORRECT' ANSWER

From your viewpoint as a student, it's crucially important that you grasp this, because it means there is rarely a single correct answer to the assignments that are set. Put bluntly, it means that no one can tell you what you should put in an assignment. Studying childhood at university, therefore, is not a case of simply knowing and remembering facts, but being able to show that you genuinely understand complexity.

However, although there may be no right or wrong answers, from an examiner's point of view, there are certainly better and worse ways of producing good assignments about childhood. The rest of this chapter is geared to help you get off to a flying start, by helping you use the teaching sessions, your experiences, your peers, your lecturers and all the activities offered on your course productively.

WHAT WILL THE TEACHING OF CHILDHOOD BE LIKE?

When people first come to university they often expect to sit in huge tiered lecture halls, simply writing down whatever 'pearls of wisdom' the lecturer utters. Studying CS/ECS is rarely like that. For a start, these courses, especially compared to subjects such as Engineering or Psychology, have relatively little scheduled class time, but instead students are expected to do more independent or directed study. In addition, you are likely to find a mixture of teaching methods used in that scheduled class time. These are outlined in Table 2.1, together with some tips for how (and how not) to approach each one.

These methods may seem less directive than those you experienced at school and college – and it can be hard not having anyone nagging you to turn up, but it's hugely important to realize that

- the lectures are important in enabling you to perform well
- tutors expect you to do much more than simply to turn up to sessions.

We'll now turn to why this is the case, and how you can make the most of what is on offer.

Table 2.1 Common teaching methods and how to approach them

Type of session	Description	Do	Don't
Lectures	Usually for large numbers of students. Will cover core ideas that everyone needs to get their heads round. May be interactive – breaking up for small-group discussion, question-and-answer sessions or debates. N.B. 'Lectures' are often used as a general term for any teaching session.	Prepare in advance. If the lecturer has set reading, get hold of it and make notes on anything you don't understand. Pick up clues about the key aims of the session. Make notes on the main points, issues, controversies and ideas and afterwards discuss with other students over coffee. Date and sort these afterwards into files for each module. Join in with discussion activities.	Simply copy down whatever the lecturer says or puts on overheads. Just turn up and hope that'll be enough.
Seminars	Tend to ask you to work on pre-prepared material. Might ask you to present your ideas, sometimes in groups.	Do your homework and go to the session prepared, even if it's not 'marked' – joining in will really help you develop your understanding before it 'counts' in assessed work. Make notes on the feedback you get, from peers as well as tutors.	Let yourself and your fellow students down by being ill prepared and not contributing to discussions.
Tutorials	Tend to be your chance to set the agenda and talk about your problems, gain feedback on your ideas when preparing an assignment or discuss your progress and devise action plans.	Prepare notes beforehand of things you want feedback on (e.g. an essay plan, uncertainties you have about core concepts or reading for a module). List questions you want to ask about to help you better understand the topic (e.g. getting clarification on a theory).	Ask procedural questions that can be answered elsewhere (e.g. word limits, deadline dates, where to hand in assignments – your course administrator or handbooks can tell you). Expect your lecturer to cover material from a lecture that you missed.
Directed study	This is like 'homework', which you do out of class contact time, although it's rarely taken in or marked. Expect to spend a lot of time on this and on more general reading round (usually called 'independent study'), as it helps you make sense of sessions and is crucial to producing good assignments.	Make sure you do it, as it will help you make the most of teaching sessions. Talk about it with other students. (See Chapter 3, 'Reading Into Writing', for guidance.)	Put it off or rely solely on formal contact time if you want to do well in your assignments

WHY GO TO LECTURES?

On any course students need to become alert to the ways in which things are done in their particular subject area. In CS/ECS courses you will need to get yourself clued in to the following ways of knowing about childhood:

- Knowing yourself.

- Knowing your lecturer.

- Knowing the subject/content.

In the rest of this chapter we'll explain what we mean, and how you can use lectures to best effect to help you build up these ways of knowing.

KNOWING YOURSELF: PERSONAL VIEWS OF CHILDHOOD

It's useful to think of learning to study childhood at university as a sort of journey. Achieving the complexity, subtlety and questioning approach to CS/ECS that we outlined at the beginning of this chapter usually means starting initially with what we know and experience at an individual, personal level. Most CS/ECS courses will, therefore, begin the course, and probably most modules, by first identifying and then questioning or challenging your own relevant personal experience in particular contexts. The following examples are designed to give you a flavour of the sorts of activities lecturers may use to help you take this initial step on the road to theorizing childhood.

Identifying personal views of the child

You will probably undertake introductory tasks and class activities that help you to identify your own opinions and views of the child-related topics lecturers are teaching. Firstly, lecturers usually want to show you that when we look at a child we may think that we all see the same thing. We don't. What we see depends on what we bring to the situation – our personal 'baggage'.

We all have values and beliefs about what is proper, right and good for children, values that usually relate to our own experiences. Often we haven't really thought about them, assuming instead that they are 'just the way things are'. Lecturers typically want you to start to see these views and opinions as 'loaded' and problematic. For this reason, it's important when studying childhood to identify and know about your own views.

Identifying your personal views and values by talking with fellow students

Here, for example, is a student talking about the age at which, in her opinion, children should start school:

We send children to school properly at five. They need to learn to read and write, and the earlier they start the better, because otherwise they'll fall behind. And no one can get by these days without being able to read and write properly.

This student was taken aback to find that another student in her discussion group was outraged at the prospect of sending children into formal education so young:

In Norway we don't force children to read and write until they're ready. They need to play and enjoy life and find out who they are and how to get along with other people first. They learn to read and write when they're about seven.

Neither student really noticed what they took for granted about children's needs, until they discussed it. This is why your peers are so important: you can all help each other begin to register the complexity of studying childhood.

Getting involved in class discussions about people's views and beliefs helps us to see how variable these are. You are on the right lines if you start to question what you previously 'knew' – or failed even to register – beforehand. Students often say studying childhood is like suddenly waking up, and hence is very different from previous study.

'It makes you think a lot more, think in different ways. There are things you accept before you come here that you don't happen to think about, unless you study this course. Things occur to me now, that I wouldn't have thought about

before – in everyday life. Like, you're watching children in society, all the time. How they're treated.'

Thinking about the words we use

You might get asked to identify your personal opinions, values and attitudes by noting your personal feelings and reactions to, say, a video clip of children, or some images.

In this example, for instance, a lecturer shows her class a video of a child with her mother, shopping in a supermarket. The child can be seen running up and down the aisles of busy shoppers, gathering armfuls of goods from the shelves and pushing the trolley in all directions.

Students write down what they see, and then compare and contrast their notes. Usually, their views vary. Some see the girl as 'naughty' and feel sorry for the mother, who they see as not being able to control her daughter, or as being subject to other shoppers' views of her 'poor' parenting skills.

A naughty little girl is banging her trolley into other people's trolleys. The poor mother is embarrassed, because everyone is staring, especially when the little girl has a tantrum.

The girl is behaving like she's spoiled: the mum should stop her. She's being a real nuisance.

Others' sympathies lie with the child.

I remember the boredom of going shopping as a child – at least this little girl is managing to liven things up! She's just having fun!

The point is that different students bring different things to analyse exactly the same incident. The difference lies in their **values, attitudes and assumptions** about what makes a 'good' mother, about how children should behave, about what children are like and how they should be treated.

Note how the words they use reveal this: '*poor* mother'; '*naughty* girl', '*just* having fun'. These words show their views of the child are far from neutral. It is, therefore, invariably a useful exercise to think carefully and critically about the words people use to describe children and childhood.

CONTINUED

Tuning in to these words helps you to see where people might be coming from when they talk, and later write, about CS/ECS topics.

When you come to write your assignments lecturers will expect you to 'define your terms' – to show that you know that there are many different ways of viewing a phenomenon, and can spell out clearly the ways in which your essay uses a word or term. We will talk more about this in later chapters, but it's important that you realize that many of the informal in-class exercises that are set encourage you to practise thinking about the ways in which words and images used to discuss and describe children and childhood are deeply loaded with significance.

Making the familiar strange

Lecturers will often get you to jot down notes about your prior knowledge of the child and childhood. You might be asked, for instance, to write down, as quickly as possible and in no particular order, all the words that spring to mind in response to the question, 'What is a child?'

'What is a child?'

Here's what some students wrote:

Innocent	Happiness	Small
Curious	Carefree	Always learning
Playful	Fun	
Vulnerable	Enthusiastic	
Cute	Loveable	
Friendly	Dependent	

The lecturers then prompted students to think about how these words, on the whole, combined to create a hugely idealized image of the child. To show how 'loaded' the words are, they asked students to think about the implications for real children.

CONTINUED

In fact, the first set of words mostly construct the child as perpetually happy, leaving no space for children to be sad (what if their pet has just died?); bored (what if they have to sit through a dull set of wedding speeches?); or knowing (what if they've been involved in bullying at school?). Among other things, this can exert a potentially huge pressure upon real children.

Students realized the extent to which the words and ideas that spring to mind to describe the notional child are often very biased, and, when taken altogether in this sort of exercise, reveal common generalizations about children. The artificiality of the exercise, which doesn't ask students to relate to 'real' children, heightens this, but it usefully shows how far adults have **abstract ideas about the meanings of childhood** that result in stereotypes about children. Often, as in this case, these ideas reflect dominant beliefs: commonly held values, attitudes and assumptions. This exercise, then, moves students' knowing from the tacit (taken for granted) to the explicit, making them question, once more, what they already think they know.

Life maps and timelines

A personal timeline

Another common exercise to get you thinking about your personal views of childhood is to get you to draw a line like the one below, asking you to mark key milestones on the line, as you moved from childhood to adulthood.

Myself as Child ———————————————— Myself as Adult

Don't enter any information you would rather not share in these sorts of exercises: lecturers are not asking you to dig up unhappy memories. People usually put things like 'started school', 'moved house', 'best friend moved', 'passed driving test', 'pet died', 'parents divorced', 'rented own flat' and so on.

When these are compared and contrasted you'll probably notice some broad similarities in childhood experience (especially if people have fairly similar backgrounds and cultures), but large discrepancies on a personal level. This helps you see the point that childhood is a relative, variable entity, dependent on an individual's personal experience. Put simply, no two childhoods are actually the same.

Timelines from childhood to adulthood

This is a similar exercise, but more general, noting the milestones many children can be expected to pass and dividing the timeline up into stages. Students put things like 'weaned', 'started walking', 'learned to read', 'went to school', 'take SATs', 'move from primary to high school', 'first date', 'able to drink alcohol', 'learned to drive', 'allowed to have sex', 'start periods', 'leave school' 'can get married', 'allowed to vote', 'first job', 'go to college' and so on.

Discussion usually focuses on a wide range of different conceptual categories that can be used to define childhood. These might include

- Biological and developmental definitions (e.g. weaned, started walking, puberty, physiological changes. These often lead to stage definitions: i.e. babyhood, toddler, middle childhood, adolescence, young adulthood).
- Institutional/educational definitions (e.g. pre-school, nursery-aged child, primary-school pupil, high-school pupil, school-leaver, college student).
- Age definitions (0–3, under 5s, 7–11, pre-teens, teenagers, young adults).
- Legal definitions (age at which allowed to have sex, drink, smoke, drive, etc.).
- Gender definitions (girlhood might be qualitatively different to boyhood).

Reflecting on personal experience usually prompts debate about the extent to which 'real' children actually conform to these definitions and norms. In particular issues around:

CONTINUED

- Social values, attitudes and beliefs about children (especially their status, how far they are seen as dependent and incompetent, or capable and independent).

- Personal beliefs about how far children 'need' to conform to these milestones.

- What happens to children who don't, or cannot, conform (e.g. how disabled children are seen when they don't meet developmental 'norms').

You need to learn to tune into the nature of these debates in each module, because they furnish you with essential information about your tutor – what they see as important, what issues they want you to understand and be able to discuss and so on.

KNOWING YOUR LECTURER AND KNOWING THE SUBJECT/CONTENT

These two things are often intertwined, as we'll show you. Lecturers will encourage you to question and interrogate taken-for-granted meanings around childhood through exploring personal values, as we have shown. Don't assume, though, that because lecturers ask for your personal experience, they want you to express unconsidered opinions in your assignments. What they want you to do is to learn to *theorize* what you say. To do well in their assignments you must get to know their expectations about theorizing material. In this sense, knowing your lecturer is not about knowing them as a person or buttering them up so they'll give you better marks, but making sure you fully understand their expectations about subject, content and how it is discussed.

This is more complicated than it sounds because every lecturer will have their own disciplinary and/or professional approach to talking academically about childhood and children. You need to cue yourself in to the ways in which they theorize the subject area. These can vary dramatically from tutor to tutor and from course to course, so it's important for you to remain sensitive to the concepts, terminology and issues they wish you to discuss in the assignments they set. You will need to use these to show that you have moved beyond personal opinion when you come to tackle your assignments, because you will be marked down if you offer an untheorized opinion.

But how do you know what each lecturer wants?

Going to lectures is the key to finding out each lecturer's theoretical approach to the subject: what counts as theory, for them, and how they define the nature of the subject or field of enquiry. You can fathom this out by thinking about the following things:

Identifying your lecturers' key course themes and issues

The first step is to make sure you grasp the *issues* each lecturer wants their students to explore. Your assignment should relate to these. Specific issues reflect the focus of the subject area of the degree, or even lecturers' individual research interests, hence they can vary immensely. Certain ones crop up in different guises, though, as common course themes, threads and key issues. Some examples of common course themes might be

- power, control and decision-making on behalf of children
- status
- children's perspectives and viewpoints
- motivation
- ownership
- families
- inclusion and equal opportunities
- play
- citizenship and participation
- parenting
- gender

- learning (formal, informal, and unintended, e.g. the hidden curriculum)

- growth and development

- autonomy

- children's rights and agency

- policy and practice

- adults' roles (professional perspectives, parents' views, censorship)

- choice

- success and failure.

Identifying your lecturers' theoretical stance to the subject area they teach

The reading list reveals any tutor's key concepts, viewpoints and approaches to studying childhood – and will equip you with the main 'tools' your tutors want you to use. We look at this in detail in the next chapter. The easiest way to begin, though, is to pay careful attention to what goes on in formal sessions. Here your lecturers will tend to introduce you to the perspectives and theories that interest them in more formal ways.

They'll tend to do this by presenting *conflicting perspectives*. On CS/ECS courses it's important to identify and talk about diverse perspectives, because this is the first stage of beginning to 'get into' any area being studied. In lectures, therefore, look out for the *key questions* each lecturer highlights or poses for you to discuss. This is where tutors really reveal the issues they want you to explore, and the concepts and terminology they want you to use. Time spent after sessions thinking carefully and making notes on the nature of these questions and debates – the big ideas – will be time well spent and improves your chances of doing well in assignments.

We'll now move on to think about how your lecturers might do this.

Introducing you to starkly different or contrasting views of the child

Many courses will introduce students to the different models, concepts or images of the child that can best be seen by comparing differences between time, place, culture and so on. Historical approaches help us see how the child was/is seen as a special category of people, increasingly regarded as essentially different from adults, and viewed in relation to other social categories, such as gender (is girlhood different from boyhood?), class (is unemployed or working-class childhood different from middle- or upper-class childhood?), ethnicity (is childhood different according to your ethnic group?). It also helps us see how far, and in what ways, childhood is viewed as being different from (or similar to) adulthood in different contexts.

Historical constructions of the child

You may be asked to think about current ideas about childhood by reflecting on historical views of the child. This is because it is argued that social and historical factors have an important bearing on the experience of being a child. We can consider what meanings adults have associated with childhood as a state of being and begin to analyse the ways in which attitudes towards children have changed and developed by looking at representations of childhood across time.

For example, we can see that the state of being a child shifts if we think about differences in how long, say, childhood lasts. In Western countries nowadays we might expect children to start to play a formal economic role at the age of 15 or so, while in the past children as young as 6 went out to work.

Furthermore, at different times childhood could be seen, for example,

- as a time of Romantic innocence, during which children should learn naturally, protected from the polluting influences of adult institutions and ideas

- as innately evil, with Evangelical adults needing to be 'cruel to be kind' to ensure that children follow the path to righteousness and proper moral conduct

- as a time in which children are like blank slates ('Tabula Rasa') waiting for adults to give them knowledge and make them learn.

Always think carefully about the questions your lecturer highlights if they present you with starkly contrasting perspectives. Do they highlight questions relating to cultural determinants (e.g. gender, class)? Or do they highlight questions relating to children's agency (children's voices, power, status)? Do they highlight questions of policy or professional practice (how can the best interests of children be served in, say, legal, health, care or educational settings)? Or do they focus on questions surrounding the representation of childhood (tensions between Romantic conceptions of the child as innocent and the child as knowing, debates about portrayals of the child in poetry, comics or other media)?

Recognizing the diversity of Childhood/Early Childhood Studies as a subject area

Activities and reading that help students think about the variable ways in which childhood can be interpreted are important to CS/ECS as an emergent field. Lecturers often set such activities because they help students to perceive key questions about the meanings of childhood. Once more, seeing different points of view can help learners recognize, sharply and often with a shock or a jolt, how they think and feel about the 'reality' of childhood today. It makes us ask questions such as

- What makes someone seem childish or childlike?

- What behaviour is regarded as 'appropriate' for children?

- What is a child's nature really like? (Are children innately evil or inherently good?)

- Who 'owns' childhood and who governs it? How should children be treated?

- What is good for children?

All this draws attention to the crucial importance of *adults'* ideas about the meanings of childhood, which may not be what you expect to be studying. In fact, many of the questions on CS/ECS courses revolve around how adults see children: the meanings they ascribe to them and the ways in which they treat them.

It's worth emphasizing, that, as a consequence, academic study of childhood often focuses on *representations*, stories and concepts – ideas – about the child (in line with disciplines such as sociology, English and cultural studies), as well as focusing (like disciplines such as education or psychology) on the child or children per se. You are looking for the hidden meanings, if you like, whether the focus of study is representational art about children, or products for children (paintings, fiction, magazines) or 'real-life' interview data (professionals, parents or children talking about childhood).

PERSPECTIVES ON CHILDHOOD

Most courses nowadays will have a module that introduces varying views of the child, and highlights diverse perspectives on the meanings associated with childhood. Such modules aim to get you thinking about the hugely different ways in which childhood as an idea can be seen.

The words lecturers will probably use to highlight this common theme include

perspectives	paradigms
views	conceptions
images	ideologies
models	ideas
theories	notions
versions	discourses
constructions	perceptions
concepts	interpretations . . . of childhood.

Identifying the key issues within a module

Getting to know your lecturer also means tuning in to how far your lecturer is interested in studying children as 'real' embodied individuals, perhaps in particular professional contexts or settings, or how far they expect you to explore more general ideas about concepts of childhood in a more abstract sense. Again, thinking about the focus of their lectures and the key debates or questions they expect you to be able (eventually) to discuss and theorize in a scholarly, academic manner in your assignment will give you a good idea. They will usually start, however, by getting you to simply see that there is a debate to be had.

Often they refer to key debates, or even set up debates for you to hold among yourselves in class. Recognizing these is the key to success.

WORKED EXAMPLE 1

Identifying the key issues

A lecturer teaching Child Development was keen to introduce her students to 'great' researchers: people, like Piaget, who had conducted experimental research, observing children and drawing up theoretical viewpoints. She was concerned, however, that because a lot of her students would feel that they 'already knew' about these theories from previous courses, they would tend to simply regurgitate the researchers' accounts of the 'ages and stages' in the assignment they produced. This was not at all what she wanted – instead she expected her students to **stand back and question** psychologists' interpretations of the factors that impact on children's development. This, for her, was theory.

To highlight this she based her lectures on key themes, such as the extent to which various theorists saw the role and relative importance of genetic or environmental factors in children's development. In sessions she encouraged students to compare and contrast different theorists' views of the ways in which children are understood to develop, change, grow and make sense of the world. The questions she raised in sessions surrounded

- How do different researchers and theorists (Locke, Skinner, Bandura, Vygotsky, Freud, Piaget) believe that children learn?

- How does each explain children's emotional, social and intellectual growth?

The essay title she set was 'Piaget was a psychologist who explored factors that impact on children's development. Discuss his findings in the light of relevant literature.' Poor essays were those in which students simply gathered and copied down information about Piaget's stages. Essays that received good marks discussed Piaget's ideas by recognizing them as part of a **debate** about the relative importance of nature and nurture.

WORKED EXAMPLE 2

A lecturer teaching Childhood and Human Rights wanted to encourage students to think about the complexities involved in coming to decisions which could be deemed to be 'in the best interests of the child'. After outlining the series of markers laid down by the UN Convention, her sessions focused on how children are constructed in the minds of adults and the relationship between this and the implications for social policy and practice in the care, education and health of children within both the family and the wider community.

In sessions she got students to discuss and debate issues of power: who holds it, how it is accessed, what is the commitment to power sharing. One debate, for example, focused on the 'Gillick Case', which students were asked to read about before the session. The lecturer asked one group to make the case that girls under the age of 16 should have access to contraception without their parents' knowledge. She asked the other group to put the view that this would encourage promiscuity and the promotion of under-age sex to people who might not be emotionally ready.

In this way the lecturer encouraged students to think about who they thought should decide and why, as a first step to identify the issue and perceiving the debate, which hinges essentially upon different views of the child. She was not looking, ultimately, for a gut-response or an opinion, but for a reasoned response, acknowledging different points of view. Other sessions were used to model similar debates, by presenting different perspectives on whether a disabled child's 'best interests' would be served by attending a special or a mainstream school, and on whether conjoined twins should be separated, if the operation risks the result of only one twin's survival.

The lecturer hoped that by setting up in-class debates students would be clear that she would give very low marks to an assignment that simply regurgitated the principles of the UN Convention, and expected essays to discuss and debate the complexities and problems involved in decision-making on children's behalf. The next two chapters will explain the ways in which she hoped students would move beyond the

CONTINUED

broad, rather emotive debates initiated in her teaching sessions, into theorizing different perspectives via reading, but for now it's important to recognize that the sessions act as important signals to cue-sensitive students about the nature of the issues this lecturer hoped to raise.

EXPLORING POLICY ISSUES

As we've said, then, CS and ECS courses are likely to require you to study *adults'* views and assumptions on childhood, as much as study children themselves. Adults' beliefs, approaches, and the views of policy-makers are common themes on CS and ECS courses, because children's worlds and environments are heavily shaped, and constrained, by what adults want, or the ways in which adults believe children and young people should be treated.

Child-centred consultation (seeking children's views and seeing them as people *now* rather than as just miniature adults-in-the-making) may well be another issue to emerge in different areas within your course. The questions to emerge here might be

- How can you, in policy terms, balance the tensions between seeking to protect children while including them in decision-making?

- Who decides what is in the child's best interest, when parents, professionals and children cannot agree?

MAKING VISITS AND RESEARCH OBSERVATIONS

Some courses will take you out into the 'real world'. Again, it's important to tune in to what specific lecturers expect if they send you out, say, into early years settings, or to interview parents or professionals, or work with children themselves.

Consider the following case study, which focuses on the in-class discussions that emerged from a visit to early years settings. We'll present the visit itself in photos, so that you can see what we're talking about, and hear the sorts of questions the lecturer wanted her students to think about and start to identify. These questions offer you a model of asking yourself questions, an important key to successful study. Once more, this is a process you'll learn through participating in the sessions and activities lecturers make available.

Worked example: Comparing and contrasting images of the child in school

An ECS lecturer on a module entitled 'Care & Education in Context' wanted her students to think about professionals' perspectives on childhood and how far different views of the child impacted on the services made available for the very young. First she asked her students to describe what they saw in two different settings in which children aged between 3 and 6 received care and education. She asked them to bring written responses to each photograph (Figure 2.1), which is of the entrance halls of the schools concerned. You can see the instructions and trigger questions she asked, together with one student's responses, in the box below.

Describe what you see in both pictures

Picture A: Children have drawn their own pictures of themselves. They have written their own names. The pegs have their own bags and coats on them, all of which are different. It looks disordered and colourful. There's a collage above on the wall done by children.

Picture B: Each name sticker is on a very symmetrical peg. Every sticker has been done professionally on card, they are all the same size and have a glossy image of an animal. Adults have written the child's full name on each. The pegs have got the children's coats on. Some bags are different, but most are peg bags made identically in the same material as used for uniforms. It look quite orderly. There are certificates on the wall.

How are they the same?

Both identify the children and name them as individuals. They are the space where children bring and leave their own possessions. They both seem to be in the entrance hall. Both have adult versions of writing.

CONTINUED

How are they different?

The first one children have drawn and labelled their own space, and have done a representation of themselves to identify this. Emphasis on drawing rather than writing. They recognize through a picture they have drawn. The second one is not a picture of their own making. The first one has a jumble of different items, whereas the second one has a very similar set of items, that all look like school possessions. The first one offers the child a chance to develop their own space. But the second one is done by the adult.

What do you think adults in each setting would say are the reasons why they have developed their particular entrance area the way they have?

In the first one they want to encourage the children to bring what they have to the school, to feel a sense of belonging and be part of the school and to recognize their difference. To welcome diversity and recognize that you are an individual.

In the second the setting is saying this is how we do things here. These are the routines that help children to become part of this school. This is levelling the children, protecting them from difference and sharing the school identity and community.

What do you think the adults in each setting feel is important for children's learning?

In the first setting they value children learning about themselves as individuals, how they are different from each other, taking some measure of control of their space and environment, learning to value and recognize difference. They want them to practise emergent writing, but it's OK to have a go, even if it doesn't look perfect.

The second setting values conformity to the expectations of others, to learn that they are not special or unique, to view adults as giving a right model and to meet adults' expectations in school, to achieve high standards by learning from best examples, to follow an expert, that there is only one way that is right that you should strive to reach.

Figure 2.1 Images of early years settings

You can see how the trigger questions have helped the student move beyond simple description towards first-stage analysis, by encouraging them to identify the issues that begin to emerge when you consciously set out to compare and contrast different perspectives on childhood.

Learning to ask yourself questions about why things are as they are, or why people hold certain values, or how people construct and reveal views of children's needs is essential to studying CS/ECS. If you get into the habit of using sessions to tap in to the relevant issues, identifying the 'big questions' and rehearsing your responses to different ways of addressing them, you should be well placed to successfully tackle the reading and the assignment. This is because you will start to see what *you* need to know and be able to do on each module, which will enable you to take fruitful next steps.

LOOK FOR ISSUES NOT ANSWERS: 'IT DEPENDS'

In short, your course is likely not to give you 'answers' but to *raise issues*. CS/ECS is, increasingly, all about problematizing what can be made to sound extremely easy: doing the right thing by our children, whether as carers, policy-makers, educators or parents. You will no doubt study provision, policy and legislation on your course, but you must learn to adopt a critical, academic eye when you look at these, too. Again and again, you should realize that whatever is done on behalf of children is far from simple: it all depends on how you see it.

It's therefore very important to perceive the steps that help you to become critical and analytical when studying children and childhood. 'Critical' in this context does not mean you have to disagree with everything (although we have tried to suggest this is a useful first step), it means weighing up and thinking questioningly about other people's ideas, looking for the meanings beneath the surface, contrasting different interpretations and people's values, attitudes, principles and assumptions about children, childhood and children's worlds. It means tuning in to the ways in which people disagree, and, even more importantly, thinking about the reasons why they disagree. It means identifying complex and untidy issues, and logically following through and teasing out what different viewpoints might mean. It means always asking 'why?'

The next chapter helps you to see the role of further reading to extend this process of critical enquiry.

Chapter 3

Reading Into Writing

This chapter will unpack why tutors give you reading lists and will often set particular papers, books or chapters for you to absorb before, during or after teaching sessions. It will help you use them to guide your reading about childhood. The chapter will show, through worked examples, the ways in which secondary texts are the students' windows onto, and access into, an academic, authoritative debate.

GETTING TO GRIPS WITH WHY READING MATTERS SO MUCH ON CS/ECS DEGREES

Chapter 2 highlighted that CS/ECS courses explore how views and opinions about children and childhood are not fixed, but vary according to lots of different factors. However, to do well on your CS/ECS course you need to be able to think and write academically, not just recognize that everyone sees childhood in different ways. This will involve taking hold not just of the language of academic discourse, but also the range and diversity of ideas, concepts, ideologies and standpoints that exist around childhood. This crucially rests upon a student's *reading*.

Reading is a hugely important activity on any degree course. Once you understand why it is important and can pinpoint what you are trying to achieve by 'reading round' a topic, you will be in a position to develop your own approach to the research that needs to be done in order to write a successful assignment. This chapter offers practical examples of effective reading strategies used by students on their CS/ECS courses and relates them directly to the act of student writing. Above all, by the end of this chapter we hope you'll see that reading and writing are ongoing and integrated aspects of learning, rather than something you do only at the end of a module when you have to physically produce the assignment.

LEARNING HOW TO SEE THE SIGNIFICANCE OF THE READING THAT TUTORS SET FOR YOU

We said in Chapter 2 that you need to tune in to each tutor's perspective by considering the debates, key questions and issues they highlight in taught sessions. You can also learn a huge amount about how they view the topic from the reading that they ask you to do. It's vital that you engage with this, as it's another crucial aspect of getting to know your tutor and being sure that your work eventually meets their expectations.

Reading lists and the chapters, articles or books set for particular teaching sessions introduce you to and immerse you in academic debates about the sorts of ideas and issues that the lecturer wants you to grasp. They show you a range of theoretical frameworks or approaches or beliefs, any of which can be used as lenses through which to view different aspects of childhood. In short, they act as a 'toolkit of ideas' which enable you to perceive different perspectives; compare, contrast and consider the implications of different viewpoints on childhood; and make points yourself when writing about a topic. Tutors will expect you to use these terms and concepts when you prepare your assignment. Let's think about how and why you should invest a lot of time in reading.

DOING THE READING IN PREPARATION FOR SEMINARS AND TEACHING SESSIONS

When lecturers set reading that they want you to do before a session, they typically do so to help you make sense of the literature you need to know about before you can come to understand their topic area. If they say that reading a specific text is required or essential, they mean it. Such readings are going to be those that offer the greatest insight into a topic. Lecturers will guide you to see the set reading's significance, and help you to perceive the questions and issues raised by reading theory. Don't waste this opportunity – it's your chance to rehearse your ideas and understandings before they 'count' in written assignments. After reading, ask about anything you don't understand, and check for yourself whether you've got the right end of the stick by talking it through with peers and tutors.

In the box below, for example, is a concrete illustration of how lecturers might use theoretical reading to help you move beyond common-sense views of an issue by encouraging you to *use* (rather than just obtain) theory. This is often what they want you to do in your assignments – so use every chance you have to rehearse this as the module unfolds.

WORKED EXAMPLES

Perspectives on childhood: comparing theoretical viewpoints

In a key introductory module designed to highlight the range and diversity of different views of the child, students were asked to read two brief extracts, reproduced in the module guide, that were drawn from academic articles. These extracts both discussed the position of the child in the family, but each took a markedly different standpoint, which is precisely why the lecturers had set them for students to consider.

- One outlined Postman's ideas, and was set because it represented 'New Right' ideology, by implicitly assuming that the 'best' family form is middle-class, patriarchal, with two parents and so on. It expressed the view that such family structures are fundamental mechanisms that allow for the protection and preservation of a hallowed form of childhood innocence that children need in order to feel special and flourish.

- The other drew attention to Holt's ideas, who argued that such an outwardly 'perfect' childhood and family life may actually disguise a potentially oppressive childhood experience, in which children may have few rights, are infrequently listened to, and are consigned to a social position of inferiority and limitation, in which they are supposed to appear relentlessly happy. Childhood, according to Holt, might be experienced as a prison, rather than a Romantic garden.

In the teaching session the lecturers assumed that the students had read and reflected on the extracts. They asked students to briefly discuss each theorist's viewpoint in small groups, by comparing and contrasting their perspectives and the way that the articles defined the terms 'child' and 'family'.

CONTINUED

Then they asked students to *use and apply* these viewpoints to analyse an extremely conservative photograph of a family, which depicted father and mother posing with their arms round their two children, a boy (carrying a football) and a girl (carrying a book). Because of their view of childhood and the family, each theorist is likely to interpret aspects of this image differently.

- One is likely to see the father's arm as a protective shield around his child's shoulders, while the other is likely to regard the father's arm as a restraint that is keeping the child in its lowly place.

- One is likely to view the children's neat clothes as a sign of the loving family's care and provision for its children, the other may see the children's clothes as signs of enforced conformity and denial of individual expression, so the children are seen as possessions and showpieces, rather than people with their own views and opinions.

- One might see the gender roles as a mark of natural normality, the other might see them as representing subservience and oppressive forms of dominance and expectation within the family dynamic.

The questions raised by the lecturers in the plenary discussion related to issues of power, choice, autonomy and control. Again, this is an instance in which you can pick up important cues about the themes and issues tutors regard as important – you should tap into them as you develop your assignment. Always ask yourself: what ideas, issues and questions does the lecturer want me to get out of this reading?

WHAT IS AN ARGUMENT?

To be able to *use* any given theory, as in the case above, you need to have developed a firm grasp of the main arguments each theorist puts forward or asserts – the big ideas and ways of defining terms. Try to make notes, therefore, which précis or summarize a theorist's arguments – the main way they see things or the 'take' they have on something, their theoretical standpoint. This will often mean 'reading into' what they say and how they say it, because their assumptions might be tacit. For instance, if you were to read Neil Postman's *The Disappearance of Childhood* (1983) you need to identify his ideological perspective. He doesn't tell you what it is, or that his views could be considered extreme in any way. Instead, he assumes that the reader shares his values, position and statements about 'the family', his analysis of society, children's needs and adults' rights. In short, he argues that childhood is disappearing and highlights why, for him, this is a bad thing, but he does this from his own perspective – his values, attitudes and assumptions. (Our summary can be seen in the first two bullets in the above box as an example of précising an argument or perspective.)

Note, too, that you're often looking for *sets of ideas* rather than individual people's *personal* views when you are reading. In this case, for example, it didn't matter to the lecturer which theorist (specific person) you used when it came to producing your final assignment. Instead, Postman and Holt were simply used at one point as *illustrations* of a particular viewpoint, or as representing a dominant set of ideas about views of the child in the family. You could have used a range of others, as long as they represented diverse views and standpoints. In short, in order to write about the key concepts of any module, you need to be able to summarize and synthesize a whole body of academic writing succinctly.

KEEPING GOOD NOTES BY ASKING YOURSELF QUESTIONS AS YOU READ: READING WITH A PEN

Just as it's really unhelpful to simply copy down what someone says in a lecture, it's also not much use just sitting in front of a book. To profit from reading, it's useful to think of it as an activity or conversation, in which you, as well as the writer of the book or article, has an important part to play.

Creating good notes takes time, as it needs to be done slowly and steadily. Making effective notes that summarize the main viewpoint of the theory that you read will ensure that you read for understanding, rather than just gathering hordes of material which you haven't thought about at all. Everyone has made photocopies of articles and chapters, meaning to read them, but then put them in a file, or under the bed, and forgotten about them until the assignment is due. Instead, to make sure you don't have to panic or rush, read them and make notes about them *just after* you copy them, outlining the arguments – the main ideas – comparing and contrasting them with other things you have read, reading between the lines and highlighting illustrative quotes. This will also help you to avoid plagiarizing by accident (there is more on this in the next chapter).

Make effective notes by *asking questions* about the material you're going through when reading, by trying to group and categorize perspectives on a topic, rather than just copying chunks out. For instance, children's reading of comics and magazines is sometimes a focus in articles and books on literacy. When reading these articles or books, one of the key questions you might ask yourself is whether the writers see comic and magazine reading as a good or bad thing. Further, asking why they think that and whether there are any clues to that in what you read, should help you to establish that there are a number of perspectives here that can be grouped, ranging from seeing comics as a way of creating literacy through to undermining it.

If you write down what you find out in response to the questions, *doing* something with the information, you're going to have valuable notes that you can use to write your assignment. You're also going to have a set of reminders to yourself about what you don't really understand, which will help you make the most of teaching sessions and tutors.

Asking questions, then, gives you a sense of wanting to find out more, wanting to go into more depth, wanting to explore, which are all good ways of approaching reading. This is what your lecturers want you to do. Let's look at a concrete example of what we mean by this.

WORKED EXAMPLE

Reading more about the care and education of young children

Imagine you have been asked, for your assignment, to consider the issues surrounding the question: 'What counts as "quality curricula" in early years education?' You would set out to research (read about) different early years approaches – building on what the teaching sessions covered. In doing your reading, though, you should not set out to gather simply factual information about each of these approaches and then say (describe) what Forest Schools, Reggio Emilia, Portage, Highscope and the Foundation Stage in the UK do. Instead you should think *why* these approaches have developed as they have and what they reveal about the views of children's needs that are embedded within them.

So, what specific questions might you look to answer or address when you're doing this reading research? You might ask, for instance:

- What are the underpinning values, attitudes and beliefs about children's and practitioners' roles and responsibilities on which this curriculum approach is based?
- What factors that impact on children's development are relevant to this curriculum approach?
- What tensions and challenges can you identify in this approach for practice (issues)?

Having specific questions in mind will mean that you read with a purpose. Summarizing each approach in a bank of notes under these headings will help you to perceive the similarities and differences, and possible tensions, between the various perspectives. This is fundamental to you being able to develop an argument in response to the question, which wants you to explore the issue of competing definitions of 'quality' in this context.

What do tutors mean by 'defining the terms you use in your essay'?

Another way of looking at this is to consider that in order to write about perspectives on 'quality' you need to be able to define the term 'quality'. A dictionary definition here is simply not good enough, because it will be too broad. What the lecturer actually wants to see is that you have understood that definitions of quality vary according (in this case) to different perspectives on education and views of the child that underpin each philosophical approach. The lecturer here expects you to make points about different views of 'quality' – which you can only get by further reading on the topic of early years curricula approaches and reading with a pen.

Reading further will help you to develop ideas and perceive the issues

If, furthermore, you research different perspectives on a range of curricula approaches you can then begin to ask more complex and sophisticated questions by comparing and contrasting your notes.

Key issues will then begin to emerge from your reading (e.g. views of the child as apprentice or dependent and unskilled versus the child as an autonomous active learner). Alternatively, your reading may reveal whether an approach regards letting children choose how they want to play and what they want to learn about is a waste of time or not. A further question might then be, 'What "side effects" might the hidden curriculum have?, or 'Is the process of learning actually more influential than the content?' All of these will be answered differently by different philosophies and theorists, relate to views of 'quality' education, and can form the basis of your writing – becoming points to develop, or possible angles you might take on the subject.

We will discuss how to develop the focus for your assignment in the next chapter, but for now it's important to emphasize how reading for understanding is essential, as it establishes the bedrock of your thinking.

Regardless of the original question, a similar range of perspectives or 'lenses' or 'ways' of viewing may well emerge, creating a basic toolkit of ideas useful in most learning situations. Reading enables you to become familiar with this toolkit and also more confident and authoritative in your ability to explore, interpret and recognize controversies and tensions within and between them.

As one student puts it, this can be quite different from former reading experiences:

*At college, you were given all the criteria, but it's more explicit. I mean – you really can't go wrong. You know all you have to do is put in the things they tell you. If that goes in, then really, you're going to pass. But [at university] it's like, well, you've got the criteria, but you've got to get an angle. You've got to look into it more – **much** more. It's really affected the way I'm going about reading.*

This student now sees reading as a matter of 'looking into' something, rather than gathering things to 'put in'. Students who do well in assignments tend to see the whole business of information literacy in this way – they try to make sense of what they read and forge it into something new.

GOOD RECORDING HABITS WHEN YOU READ

Along with keeping good notes you should develop the habit of putting down all the bibliographic details of the book that you have been looking at, as the reading lists below do. While there are a number of different ways of doing this most universities use the Harvard system. Find out what your university uses and start to write down book details in this format now. It will swiftly become automatic. This means that you will have created a bibliography you can use for your assignment.

Along with the full bibliographic details, you could make note of direct quotes that you feel are key ones, with page references (which you will also need for the final assignment). Put them in quotation marks and put your own ideas in something like square brackets, just so that you don't mix them up and accidentally plagiarize.

Finally, keeping these details as either a card index, or on disk means that you can update it easily as your reading develops. Keeping records like this means that every bit of reading you do will be remembered, and so can be referred back to for assignments all the way through your degree, so nothing is ever wasted. It also allows you to see where you have been, mapping out your journey through academic reading.

'I DON'T KNOW WHERE TO START – THERE SEEMS TO BE SO MUCH MATERIAL'

A key difficulty experienced by many students is feeling overwhelmed by the amount of reading material there is in the library, and by the length of the reading lists. The scale of both tells you that reading your way into a topic area is, from the academic's viewpoint, absolutely vital. However, don't panic, or put reading off. Most people feel 'lost' at first, so talk to your peers about reading and research. They will feel the same as you and you can help one another.

Writing an essay at university is so different! They expect you to use the library, the journals. I'd definitely never done anything like that! At first I was lost, I'd no idea. I didn't know what they expected of me.

Also, take heart – you will learn to read strategically, as well as widely, which will make the reading more manageable. Here, for example, are a couple of experienced students talking about what they try to do when they set about reading:

Student A: *I don't read every word any more, but you're trying to pick out key points. You try to figure out what they think.*

Student B: *I look for someone with the same views as myself. And then I look for someone with a contrasting view.*

They are talking about reading with a purpose – looking for different perspectives, as we flag up above. Instead of reading to answer the question, they're reading to quite consciously 'open up more questions'.

I'm finding that it's not straightforward sort of information, it's more opening up areas of interest. For example, at college we took an area of child development, and we did it in the first module at university, but we did it from the view of people I'd never even heard of! Because at college we didn't think about it like that. Here, I'm going to the library and looking at all these books – I've bought books hand over fist! Because as I'm reading I do a comparison, and I've been thinking 'Well, they're all on children's development in school, but that one's dead different to that one!' So it sort of opens up. And then you read the references of one book and it just gets bigger and bigger. Because what I'm trying to do is keep more broad, in an attempt to understand how they compare, or how they oppose each other. And that's changing what I already knew, so that it's changing all the time. That's what I'm trying to do.

This is a very useful thing to do when you're reading – it means you're setting out to try to group or categorize perspectives, as we mention above. You can do this by deliberately looking for people who are for and against something, and ask yourself 'on what grounds do they base their views and assumptions?' Once you've found different perspectives and definitions, you can then begin to focus down by analysing the possible reasons for their different outlooks.

READING INTO READING LISTS

When you go to the library, if you do feel swamped by the amount of texts available, make sure you go armed with the reading lists you have been given. Don't despair if you can't find the precise book they suggest; get clues from them and use them laterally.

On a straightforward and immediate level you can learn a lot about a tutor's expectations and outlook on the material simply by skimming the reading list. Compare and contrast the examples below, for instance. You can tell a lot just from the unit descriptors and from the books that have been chosen. It's important to learn to ask yourself key questions about the reading lists to identify the lecturer's particular 'take' on a topic. What is their approach to the subject matter? What discipline are they part of? Which section of the library are these books in? What is their Dewey number? What does the module descriptor suggest are the main ideas of the module?

WORKED EXAMPLE

Module title: Where the Hobgoblins Are

Synopsis: For some children the hobgoblins were real, for others they were fairies and for some they were social issues to be tackled. This unit seeks to use first hand archival material to develop the narrative as seen through the eyes of children in times past.

Indicative reading

History as subject/nature of history

Jordanova, L. (2000) *History in Practice*. Arnold

Marwick, A. (2001) *The New Nature of History: Knowledge, Evidence, Language*. Palgrave

Samuel, R. and Thompson, P. (eds) (1990) *The Myths We Live By*. Routledge

Methodology

Fines, J. (1990) *Reading Historical Documents*. Blackwell

CONTINUED

Context

Long, J. (1999) *Conversations in Cold Rooms: Women Work & Poverty in the 19th Century*. Northumberland Royal Historical Society/Boydell Press

Ward, T. and Ward, C. (1991) *Images of Childhood in Old Postcards*. Sutton

Narratives

Thompson, T. (1981) *Edwardian Childhood*. RKP

Warner, M. (1998) *No Go the Bogeyman: Scaring, Lulling and Making Mock*. Vintage

Warner, M. (1994) *From Beast to the Blonde: On Fairy Tales and their Tellers*. Vintage

Documents

Newcastle upon Tyne Archive Materials

You can tell from this reading list that:

- the main approach to subject matter is historical – the lecturer is keen to introduce students to historical ways of approaching and researching childhood
- checking the catalogue shows that these texts are shelved in Dewey number 704 (folklore, fear, devils and monsters); and Dewey number 930 (different histories – women, oral, memory, history-philosophy)
- the lecturer is interested in narratives and representations of child-hood in the past, with the different versions of stories that were told
- the main ideas are around the relative nature of representation and who controls and tells the stories. This is the toolkit of ideas
- Finally, the lecturer takes students to research primary material based in archives (e.g. school records) to see if and how children's voices are present and how children are viewed and recorded in this material.

WORKED EXAMPLE

Module title: Promoting Children's Health & Development

This is a year-long unit, with part one taught by one tutor, and part two by another. The different perspective of each tutor is revealed in the reading lists they suggest.

The first part is taught by a Social Work tutor, and focuses on family matters and parenting. It gets students to explore values in relation to these topics. The toolkit of ideas for this unit will need, therefore, to come from concepts about definitions of family, agencies that work with families and notions of effective practice. Checking the catalogue, these books are based around Dewey numbers 362 and 301, broadly located within sociology and focusing on issues like teenage pregnancy, family violence and family mediation.

Barnes, P. (1995) *Personal, Social and Emotional Development of Children*. Open University Press

Bernardes, J. (1997) *Family Studies – An Introduction*. Routledge

Booth, T. and Booth, W. (1994) *Parenting Under Pressure*. Open University Press

Brannen, J. and O'Brien, M. (eds) (1996) *Children in Families: Research and Policy*. Falmer

Campion, M. J. (1995) *Who's Fit to Be a Parent?* Routledge

Daniel, B. et al. (1998) *Child Development for Child Care and Protection Workers*. Jessica Kingsley

Frost, N. et al. (1996) *Home Start and the Delivery of Family Support*. Homestart UK

Gilham, B. (1997) *The Facts About Teenage Pregnancies*. Cassell

Hester, M. et al. (2000) *Making an Impact – Children and Domestic Violence*. Jessica Kingsley.

Makins, V. (1997) *Not Just a Nursery – Multi Agency Early Years Centre in Action*. NCB

CONTINUED

The second part is taught by a former Health Visitor, and reflects a focus on raising questions around definitions of children's health. A strong emphasis is placed on how child health is viewed in the 21st century. Students are encouraged to explore 'health' and 'development' from the perspective of the child, parent and professional. This will help students to critically reflect on and evaluate strategies and interventions to maximize the health and development of the young child. It raises issues to do with definition and tensions around the 'best' interest of different groupings. This is also reflected in the Dewey numbers and in the theme and topics covered by texts in that part of the library.

Doorbar, P. and McClarey, P. (1999) *Ouch! Sort it Out: Children's Experiences of Pain*. RCN

Goldman, A. (1999) *Care of the Dying Child*. Oxford University Press

Mayall, B. (1996) *Children, Health and the Social Order.* Open University Press

Putnam, R. D. (2000) *Bowling Alone: The Collapse and Revival of American Community*. Simon and Schuster

Scriven, A. and Orme, J. (2001) *Health Promotion: Professional Perspectives*, 2nd edn. Palgrave/Open University

Seedhouse, D. (2001) *Health: The Foundations for Achievement*. Wiley

Spencer, N. J. and Nicholas, J. (2000) *Poverty and Child Health*. 2nd edn. Radcliffe

Unwin, N. et al. (1997) *An Introductory Study Guide to Public Health and Epidemiology*. Open University

Wyse, D. and Hawtin, A. (2000) *Children: A Multi Professional Perspective*. Arnold

The toolkit of ideas and concepts this lecturer expects will need to draw on the issues of challenges and tensions between different professional perspectives on health in this literature.

Module title : Studying Childhood in Context

You can tell from this reading list that the tutor is interested in issues to do with the media effects debates, and wants students to explore the ways in which children and young people are regarded as passively consuming or actively interpreting television and other media. The Dewey numbers are largely at the start of the 300s, e.g. 301.16, again in the broad area of sociology.

Bazalgette, C. and Buckingham, D. (1995) *In Front of the Children*. British Film Institute

Buckingham, D. (1993) *Children Talking Television: The Making of Television Literacy*. Falmer Press

Buckingham, D. (1999) *Children's Television in Britain: History, Discourse and Policy*. British Film Institute

Mayall, B. (ed.) (1994) *Children's Childhoods: Observed and Experienced*. Falmer Press

McRobbie, A. (1991) *Feminism and Youth Culture: from Jackie to Just Seventeen*. Macmillan Education

Middleton, S. et al. (eds) (1994) *Family Fortunes: Pressures on Parents and Children in the 1990s*. CPAG

Robinson, M. (1997) *Children Reading Print and Television*. Falmer Press

Seiter, E. (1995) *Sold Separately: Children and Parents in Consumer Culture*. Rutgers UP

Styles, M. et al. (eds) (1996) *Voices Off*. Cassell

Walkerdine, V. (1999) 'Violent Boys and Precocious Girls: regulating childhood at the end of the millenium'. *Contemporary Issues in Early Childhood*, 1 (1), 3–23

The toolkit of ideas would be about the active agency and viewing – children as sense-makers.

WHY REFERENCE?

Having read a wide range of books, how will you be using them in assignments? Primarily, they will appear as references. The requirement to reference your work may be a new one and can be daunting, as this student remembers:

We were never told at college how to reference journals. That bit terrified us [me].

However, to do well in your assignments you **do** need to refer to a wide range of secondary reading, again emphasizing how important reading is.

This is linked to the way that tutors look for a reasoned and balanced argument in your assignments. Referencing is part of that as it shows that all the comments you make are qualified ('backed up' and 'substantiated' are other common terms tutors use) and that you appreciate that issues can be viewed from different perspectives.

The way to support your reasoned and balanced argument in academic writing is to reference 'evidence', 'support' or 'perspectives', as the examples of academic writing in the box below imply.

General conversation	Academic writing
'It stands to reason'	'The evidence would suggest . . . '
'Everyone would agree'	'There is extensive support for . . . '
'It is blatantly obvious'	'There is considerable evidence to support the view . . . '
'It's clear to me'	
'Children need . . . '	'In conclusion, my personal perspective on this issue would be . . . '

This 'evidence' is some of the material gleaned from your reading. In your own work, then, wide reading of reliable and authoritative texts is demonstrated by incorporating into the body of the assignment summaries of the ideas these contain and direct illustrative quotations. This is when you use 'people in brackets' (of which more in the next chapter) – a conventional way of demonstrating the theoretical reading you have done.

EVIDENCE AND AUTHORITY

Of course, as we suggest above, it does matter *what* you read, too. Some sources will be more reliable and esteemed than others and you have to be very aware of this when gathering your evidence. The following example as to why some sources can be regarded as more authoritative than others illustrates the point in everyday terms:

> Imagine you're trying to decide where to go on holiday. You've decided you want somewhere warm, for two weeks and you're on a fixed budget. Where would you go/who would you ask to help you decide where to go? How reliable would this evidence be? What would give it authority? In what ways might it be unreliable?

In this example it's quite easy to see that some people you could consult will know less or be more biased than others. But telling the difference between a useful academic source and one that is less so can be more challenging. To give you some more pointers, consider the difference between the two following statements:

'Children deserve the best in life, and their parents should buy them good books'

and

' . . . definitions are controlled by their purpose. There can be, therefore, no single definition of "Children's Literature". What is regarded as a "good" book might be "good" in the sense in which the currently dominant/literary/academic establishment prescribes; "good" in terms of effectiveness for education, language acquisition, or socialisation or for entertainment for a specific child or group of children in general or specific circumstances; or "good" in some moral or political sense; or "good" in a therapeutic sense. "Good" as an abstract and "good for" as a practical application are constantly in conflict in judgements about children's literature.' (Hunt, 1994, pp. 42–43)

The first statement is very sweeping and takes a lot of things and values for granted, while the second shows that definitions of 'good' literature for children vary according to purpose, problematizing definitions of 'good' and definitions of 'childhood'. In scholarly terms, the second is much better, and, if included in your assignment, evidences authoritative wider reading.

It is also important that you look out for bias. Think about who produced what you are reading at any given point. For example, government produced websites on policy, like that for the National Curriculum, will be different from academic articles critiquing and unpacking them, or research which explores and evaluates what happens when the rhetoric is put into practice. Obviously the latter will help you engage more fully with the sorts of ideas and questions you've been studying on CS/ECS.

So, when you read, ask another set of questions, ones that focus on the relative authority of your sources. We need to think about what we read, rather than just 'put it in'. These will include a consideration of the expected audience for the source, the purpose and possible bias of the writing, its level of scholarship (there are differences between newspaper articles and academic texts, for instance), its historical and political position, the background of the author and so on.

Some good questions are:

- What is the topic?
- Who wrote it?
- When was it written?
- Why was it written?
- Who was it written for?
- How is it presented?
- How do I react to it?

So, how might these questions work out in practice? In the following example, the students were asked to read two extracts illustrating different ways of writing about the topic of parenting education or support, and to apply the questions above.

Parenting education: report on findings

Academics at Northumbria University have recently published findings from work they have carried out with parents in the North East of England who have all received support from parenting educators.

In total, 37 parents drawn from different backgrounds and with children with a range of ages and difficulties were interviewed by the two researchers, Dr Kay Sambell and Sue Miller, both senior lecturers in Childhood Studies and Care & Education. The parents were asked to talk about the different types of challenges that they had experienced in their parenting careers and the kinds of parenting education that they had received.

The authors report that all the parents, regardless of their backgrounds, family situation or social position spoke of parenting as having been one of, if not the, most challenging task they had ever undertaken. 'What emerged' say the authors 'was a picture of parents often casting around for advice and guidance, adopting trial and error approaches and wanting to do a good job, often against considerable odds. The definition of what counted as "good parenting" appeared to be influenced by trends or fashions which, in turn, highlighted the different perspectives that have existed throughout history of what children's lives "should" be like. Today, factors such as avoiding teenage pregnancy, doing well in school, or having a well paid job, are more likely to be seen as indicators of a child having had good parents than they might have been in the past or in other cultures even today.'

They continue: 'Our views of children are constantly changing and parents today are not always able to turn even to their own parents for advice, either because they are living in a different community and almost certainly because the norms and expectations of today are at some variance from those of the previous generation. Many parents spoke of the enormous support they had received from being able to discuss and reflect on their parenting situation with other parents and parent educators and to find ways of developing close and meaningful relationships with their children that they could individualise to their own situation.

The report is published as Miller, S. and Sambell, K. (2003) 'What do parents feel they need? Implications of parents' perspectives for the facilitation of parenting programmes'. *Children & Society*, 17(1), 32–44.

Out of Control Kids: Who is to blame?

Do parents need to take more responsibility for their children? How much is too much state help? Should the government do more to teach parenting skills to mums and dads or even make them attend special classes if their children are causing trouble in the community?

Jenny, 15, is a mother of Danny, 3 months. The teachers at her school want her parents to go to their parenting class to learn to be better parents. 'I didn't really know what I was letting myself in for' the high school drop out, sporting nose ring and designer t-shirt, sighed when interviewed. 'No one really tells you about sex at school, and my parents were always too embarrassed. My mum just said "Be careful" and more or less left me to find out about the facts of life from my friends and magazines. She had me when she was 17 and she's done alright.'

Jenny is thinking about going back to school to do some examina-tions. Thanks to local Labour controlled council policy, she has the right to a free place at the nursery near her home where her baby will be cared for by fully qualified staff alongside other children whose working parents pay up to £150 a week for the privilege. 'There's no way I could afford to use this nursery if the Council didn't support me,' she said. 'Maybe I can get somewhere to live on my own with Danny. My friends told me you can usually get priority if you're a teenage parent.'

Jenny's mother, Terri, 35, unemployed, lives with her partner John, also unemployed, and 3 children: Jordan (11), Kylie (8) and Jake (6). All the children have learning and behavioural difficulties. The school they attend want both parents to have help and to attend their parenting group where they can be taught some of the basics in how to bring up their children to be responsible citizens for the future.

Extract 1 is in the style of a broadsheet newspaper's overview of an academic report. It is supposed to take a broader perspective, to present the issue dispassionately, cite evidence for assertions it makes, appear non-judgemental and logically structured. It is a cooler, more objective style of writing, which uses less emotive language and more complicated words, phrases and sentences.

Extract 2 is done in a tabloid journalism style – it makes sweeping generalizations, is opinionated and judgemental (talks of 'better' parents), draws upon 'common-sense' notions (e.g. 'I was treated like this as a kid and it's never done me any harm') and displays prejudice ('Terri, 35, unemployed, lives with her partner John' . . . the implication being a train of thinking which concludes that 'no wonder the kids have problems'). It attempts to appeal to our feelings and connect with us as individuals, focusing on the individual person by quoting an individual child and mother. It is written in a subjective and campaigning style; and its main weakness is that it presents only one, exaggerated side of the story, which can be misleading.

On one level the broadsheet style is something to emulate in your writing and reading, especially at first. One student showed he was getting the right idea when he said:

That little exercise [above] was good, because it helped you to start thinking 'Well, what's this writer trying to say?' And I've been doing that now when I read books. And also it shows you what to look for when you're writing yourself. I think about having an argument differently now – I think of it as having something to say, and different viewpoints, rather than getting at someone, trying to shoot them down. And when I did my assignments, it really helped, because I tried to ask questions about where the articles were coming from, rather than just telling them what the article said. I saw that's what they wanted me to do.

Remember, though, how important it is to **read** to inform writing, to incorporate evidence, balance and authority in your work. This is where the broadsheet article misses out – it's not sufficiently scholarly in format or presentation to be handed in as an assignment.

Although the broadsheets point the way to more formal and academic kinds of writing, they do not go far enough. You need to develop an academic way of writing that is different from everyday talking and thinking, and reading academic books and journals is the only way of learning how to do this. It takes practice and feels very unfamiliar, but again, you can only learn by doing it.

READING TO GET AN ANGLE ON YOUR ESSAY

All of the points above, however, do not mean that you can't use tabloid or broadsheet stories as *inspirations* for research, or to help you focus your assignment. Here's a student talking about just that:

I look for controversies in newspapers – that gets me started asking questions, which I then follow up in the library. Like, for instance, I got the idea of doing smacking on the Children's Rights module, because there was an article on it in the papers.

LEARNING TO USE THE APPROPRIATE TERMINOLOGY

Reading strategically is also essential on a module-by-module basis because you will need to familiarize yourself with the specific terminology each lecturer uses, because this, for them, becomes shorthand for big ideas and concepts. It takes a while to immerse oneself in the terminology – but it also gets easier with time. You need to build up statement and word banks, based on the specific vocabulary or terminology you hear in lectures and find in the required reading, which will help you to develop and express an appropriate argument when writing the final assignment for a particular module. For instance, in the lectures given in relation to the module 'Studying Childhood in Context' mentioned earlier, key terms would include 'the active viewer', 'media effects' and 'constructions of childhood'.

READING INTO WRITING

To highlight the vital importance of academic reading we will now present several short worked examples of a number of different student responses to the writing task 'What do you understand by the term "the social construction of childhood"?' We will discuss how these would achieve a range of grades, and we will offer explanations of the strengths and weaknesses in each, specifically concentrating on the ways in which they evidence wider reading.

What do you understand by the term 'the social construction of childhood'?

Answer 1

My understanding of the social construction of childhood is as follows. Childhood can be seen as the period in a young persons life between dependence and independence. It may be represented as a fact of human life, with biology determining dependency on others to provide care.

Whilst immaturity and dependence may be biological facts of life, James and Prout (1990) contend that 'The way in which this immaturity is understood and made meaningful is a fact of culture' (p. 7).

They suggest that facts of culture may vary, and this can be said to make childhood a social construction. In this sense childhood is not a static, objective and universal fact of human nature, but a social construction that is both culturally and historically determined. Comparative analysis actually reveals a variety of childhoods, rather than a single, universal, cultural phenomenon. The nature of childhood varies according to the ways in which it is interpreted and different meanings are attached to it.

James, A. and Prout, A. (eds) (1990) *Constructing and Reconstructing Childhood: Contemporary Issues in the Sociological Study of Childhood.* London: Falmer Press.

Answer 2

It is very difficult to define the various social constructions of childhood. However, James and Prout define this as a 'shifting social and historical construction' (James and Prout, 1990).

Some theorists suggest that social constructions are linked to race, culture, gender, class and time. Some of the key social constructions are:

- Children as persons in their own right
- Children as innocent
- Children as vulnerable

CONTINUED

- Children as members of a distinct group

- Children as apprentices

- Children as animals.

Answer 3

The social construction of childhood is build up of a variety of different theories. I feel that the environment that the child is surrounded by and the time when the child is growing up can influence the child.

Our society treats boys and girls very differently. We treat girls like they are very delicate and precious and that they need protecting from the world. With boy's we believe that they are rough and rouged and they should do the protecting. If that's the messages of our society, children behave like that. They are social constructed.

Answer 1 would receive the best mark – promising to be in the 2:1 range. It offers a summary of the term based on wider reading and is properly referenced. It shows that the student is, via relevant reading, beginning to grasp the important key concepts, key terms and theoretical constructs, which are lacking in Answer 3, which seems to have 'just been written' without secondary reading. If there has been any reading, in Answer 3 it has clearly been of books in a totally different field, and the lecturer in this instance will wonder if the student has confused social construction theory for socialization theory, which is different. The assessor of this work would probably suspect that the student was dimly recalling 'A' level Sociology (or had looked up 'socialization' in a dictionary and not realized it was different) and had referred vaguely to some of the things she had picked up in lectures. He might bristle at being included in the sweeping and unsubstantiated statement 'we treat girls . . . '. The spelling and other mistakes also suggest to the reader that it has not been proof-read, and is carelessly produced. All of these things suggest that the student hasn't really read round sufficiently to understand the central concepts of that module. The work would receive a low mark and may not be enough to pass.

In comparison, Answer 2 is much more coherent and shows evidence of some reading, but it is less focused and less accomplished at summarizing the reading than Answer 1, so more likely to achieve a mark in the 2:2 range. It contains a list of bullet points that should be presented as a quotation, as the student has actually copied down Mills and Mills' (2000) categories, without citing the source. Lecturers will know the field so well that they will spot this and you want to avoid them thinking that you are trying to pass off Mills and Mills' ideas as your own. So although lecturers will be pleased that you have read thus far, you must take care to cite *all* the reading sources that you draw directly upon. It's best to include a list of references as in Answer 1, even for the shortest piece of writing. Furthermore, 'putting in' bullet points as we see in Answer 2 leaves the reader having to make sense of what they see, rather than the writer explaining what they understand.

In summary, then, the extracts illustrate the differences between 'common-sense', personal, opinionated writing, and that based on wider academic reading – what we call 'reading into writing'.

Chapter 4

Producing a Good Assignment

You now know that going to lectures and reading over a period of time are fundamental to producing a good assignment on CS/ECS. This chapter, though, concentrates on making sure that you actually display your learning to its best advantage when it comes to handing in an assignment.

On CS/ECS degrees you will be assessed, for the most part, via coursework of different kinds, so in this chapter we talk extensively about the process of producing good written assignments and managing your time effectively. In addition, this chapter gives guidance on exams and on what to do if things go wrong.

GETTING THE BASICS RIGHT

It is important to create the right impression when producing an assignment. Your work should look professional, and have an academic and scholarly tone similar to the authoritative texts that you've read.

With regard to layout and style, always check with tutors in case your university has particular preferences. Whether subheadings are considered appropriate varies from place to place, as does whether you can use the first person. Make sure you follow any departmental requirements too (e.g. if front sheets are needed or if you should just print on one side of the paper) so that you don't throw marks away. The list below should help to guide you.

- **Do not include any pictures on the front cover of your assignment** and especially no Clipart images of toddlers on tricycles. This is not appropriate.

- **Make sure that the information on the front cover is clear and**

thorough. Include your name and student number and other relevant information.

- **The title should be clear**. If you have a set question, use that as the title. Alternatively, if you can choose your own angle on a question, consider using a subtitle, e.g. a title like 'It's all very well to say you'll act in the best interests of the child, until you come to put that into practice. Discuss with reference to a specific context of your own choosing' might be more clearly represented as, 'It's all very well to say you'll act in the best interests of the child, until you come to put that into practice. An exploration of parents' and teachers' views of "best practice" for children with special educational needs', as this subtitle directs the assessor into your particular 'take' on the assignment.

- **Use an appropriate font in 12 point**. Times New Roman unless otherwise specified.

- **Number pages consecutively** just in case the secure fastening on your assignment breaks.

- **Leave wide enough margins** for the assessor to read your work easily and add comments.

- **Don't use document wallets**. They are awkward to get work in and out of. Imagine having to mark 300 scripts that were all in wallets.

- **Avoid using bulky cardboard files**. Work is often posted out to examiners, and again, if marking 300 pieces of work in files, just carrying them would be impossible.

- **Use side-headings as signposts to help your reader**. If you are not allowed to use subheadings, try using them to structure your work in draft form and then take them out before you hand the work in.

- **Bibliography and references** should follow the pattern that your university suggests (probably Harvard style). See below.

- **Stick to the word length**.

Drawing on and presenting your wider reading in assignments

What you hand in must show evidence of wider reading. There are some sophisticated ways of doing this, but first we'll show you some basic ways of how you can present your wider reading when you come to write your assignment.

How to refer to others' work

When you introduce an authority avoid the following:

'A quote is . . .'

or

'Berry Mayall wrote the following reference . . .'

Try instead to include 'people in brackets':

According to Kehily (2004, p. 5) 'The idea that childhood innocence should be preserved is a pervasive one and can be seen to operate on many levels.'

or, alternatively:

'The idea that childhood innocence should be preserved is a pervasive one and can be seen to operate on many levels' (Kehily, 2004, p. 5).

Quotation marks are necessary when using an author's actual words in the order they said them, i.e. if you directly quote them. When you do this you also need to include a reference to the page they said the words on. All the other bibliographic information should be put in the list of references you include at the **end** of your assignment (the bibliography).

Instead of quoting Kehily directly, though, you could summarize her views as follows:

Kchily (2004) argues that the concept of childhood innocence, as a state to be preserved, is persistent and might function on many levels.

Because you have not directly cited her words you don't need to include the page reference, but using Kehily (2004) means it's clear these are her views, put into your own words.

Useful statement bank

Other phrases you can use like this include

Kehily (2004) suggests . . .

Kehily (2004) asserts . . .

Kehily (2004) outlines . . .

Kehily (2004) puts forward
the view that . . .

Kehily (2004) assumes . . .

Kehily (2004) believes . . .

Kehily (2004) points out . . .

Kehily (2004) conjectures . . .

Kehily (2004) claims . . .

Kehily (2004) upholds the idea
that . . .

Kehily (2004) contests . . .

Kehily (2004) states . . .

Kehily (2004) maintains . . .

Kehily (2004) observes . . .

Kehily (2004) emphasizes . . .

Kehily (2004) stresses . . .

Kehily (2004) highlights . . .

Kehily (2004) contends . . .

Kehily (2004) supports the view
that . . .

The following ways of expressing and analysing your reading might also
be useful:

[X's] . . . model / philosophy / conceptual framework / ideals / beliefs /
attitude / thinking / ideas / proposals / approach . . . seem(s) based
upon the . . . hypothesis / theory / assumption / conjecture / pre-
sumption / premise / opinion / supposition / idea . . . that [children
need . . .]

Beware misquoting

This is from a student essay:

A quote from the book <u>Childhood</u> written by Chris Jenks says Childhood is conventionally seen as a time of carefree disorganized bliss . . . The bliss goes that they [children] enjoy non-serious, play-directed activities. They avoid work and serious activities at all costs . . .

Firstly, the reference is missing: it should be (Jenks, 1996). Secondly, Jenks didn't actually say this. The student has either misinterpreted, or copied it down wrongly. Further, it's unclear when the student starts talking and Jenks stops. Good records and note-taking should prevent this.

Avoid lists of rhetorical questions

The following student wrote

The word childhood presents problems, are we talking about a boy or a girl? How old are they? How long does childhood last in terms of age? 0–10? 0–14? 0–18?

They have identified key problems of definition, and are aware of the questions surrounding the definition of the word 'childhood', but need to rephrase their questions in a more authoritative manner.

A better way of expressing the same thing might be:

Defining the term 'childhood' is complex. Some definitions focus on age specificity, but there is little agreement about which ages are relevant. Other complications include diverse cultural factors and biological and social determinants, such as gender.

Always acknowledge sources

This student wrote

So what is the phenomenon of childhood itself? Is it a state of power-lessness? Or maybe a condition of secrets and shame? Is the child an innocent creature? Are children in need of protection from the adult world? Is it a period of dependency? Or maybe a period of biological, intellectual and social development?

Bits of this sound like they have come from further reading rather than being the student's own concepts and words. As nobody else is acknowledged, the tutor would worry about plagiarism.

The students above are, however, on the right lines – they perceive key questions and issues, and recognize the 'it depends' nature of knowledge. Nonetheless, their writing would be greatly improved by using 'people in brackets' effectively.

Setting out your references

At the end of your assignment you should put a list of alphabetized references. Only include authors to whom you have actually referred as a 'person in brackets' in the body of your essay.

Christensen, P. and James, A. (eds) (2000) *Research with Children: Perspectives and Practices.* London: Falmer Press.

Jenks, C. (1996) *Childhood.* London: Routledge.

National Children's Bureau Current policy issues. URL: http://www.ncb.org.uk/ [4th October 2002]

Rimmer, L. (1999) 'Family unemployment and welfare'. *Quarterly Journal of Social Affairs*, 2(3) 243–264.

Sambell, K., Miller, S. and Hodgson, S. (2001) 'Let's Get the Assessment to Drive the Learning', in Schwartz, P. and Webb, G. (eds) *Assessment: Case Studies, Experience and Practice in Higher Education*, pp. 137–143. London: Kogan Page.

A lot of students ask 'How many references should I put in?' There are no rules about this. Generally, though, tutors would be disappointed to see only one or two, but, by the same token, won't be duped if you've put lots in but not referred to them in a constructive and illuminative way in your writing.

Avoid final, absolute language

Use speculative language when writing your assignment. This shows that you realize that the definitions you've drawn on in your wider reading are relative and provisional. By incorporating secondary reading in the following way, you show these are not your personal ideas, but traceable to a range of sources. This helps you achieve an academic, theorized tone while comparing and contrasting the secondary reading. For example,

> Sambell (2004) and Gibson (2001) both suggest that [x]. On the other hand, Miller (2003) puts forward the opposite view, asserting that [y].

Furthermore, by talking about your sources or theorists in a speculative way, you'll avoid falling into the trap of sounding like you think one is right and the other wrong. For instance, you could write

- The differences between the two standpoints might be traced to . . .

- Possible ways of explaining these differences lie in . . .

- It could be suggested that these views differ because . . .

- Potential explanations for the discrepancies between these viewpoints include . . .

Editing and proof-reading

Writing an assignment is a long, ongoing process, but another straightforward aspect of getting the basics right lies in careful editing and proofreading in the later stages. It's useful to have someone else comment on your ideas, plans and drafts. If nothing else, they will help you spot careless errors and typos which, if left uncorrected, can mar the impression your work makes on a tutor. In a moment we will turn to discuss time management and suggestions for breaking down assignment writing into clear steps, but for now the important thing to realize is the need to allow ample time, not to hurry, and to allow work time to lie fallow. Sometimes, coming back to it fresh, after a little time working on something else, allows you to see it with new eyes and realize more fully its strengths and limitations, enabling you to edit it more effectively.

It is also useful to write the introduction last. This might not sound logical, but when marking, tutors often initially skim an essay before going through it thoroughly. At this point they look at the introduction, conclusion, subheadings, the list of references and the title to see where the student is coming from. Writing the introduction last, then, gives the reader an adequate gist of what you have actually done and what your argument is. Read back over your work. What have you actually written about? How can you best explain the work, clearly and pithily, in the introduction?

A hurried assignment will probably be structured and worded poorly, as you won't have had a chance to hone and refine it, something which editing and returning to it over a period of time allows you to do. Further, a piece of work handed in after writing it the night before is guaranteed to be filled with all sorts of errors, including many that proof-reading would have caught. Using a spell-checker will help. However, a spell-checker won't notice when you have spelt the word right, but have used the wrong word. Re-read your assignments.

WHAT TO DO IF LIFE GETS IN THE WAY

Stuff happens. It may mean that you can't meet your deadline for an assignment. Don't panic, but do let people know if things go wrong. You should contact the person in charge of the module for which you cannot hand in the work first. Email them and make an appointment if necessary. They will be able to tell you if you can have an extension (allowing you more time to finish the work) and what forms you might need to fill in, or what proof tutors need you to provide (e.g. a letter from your GP) to allow you to have more time.

If things are more serious and you are really struggling with *all* your work, then, if you have a personal tutor, they should be your main point of contact. Ideally, they can help with module leaders and any forms, or may refer you on to the person in charge of your degree if you need to try and re-sit a semester or even a year's worth of work. Don't let a problem build up. Don't feel you are alone. They are there to help.

Finally, you can also contact student services. There are usually sections on the university website that will lead you to learning support services or writing support units. These can offer a huge range of support, from, say, information on how best to approach certain assignments through to helping you if the information about a learning disability seems to have gone astray and tutors aren't taking it into account by giving extra time in exams.

STRUCTURING AND PLANNING YOUR ESSAY

By now you should be clear about how to get the basics right, so let's turn to the most challenging and most important part of producing your assignments, especially as far as getting good marks is concerned. Effective assignments are organized, focused, develop a *well-founded argument* based on well-assimilated wider reading, and *explore* issues. Weak assignments are ill focused, try to cover too much material, or just gather information to 'put in'. Worse still are those that are untheorized, opinionated and jumbled.

If you read on you will soon see that essay planning is *much* more complex than simply ensuring you have a beginning, middle and a conclusion.

DON'T START WRITING YOUR ASSIGNMENT AT THE LAST MINUTE!

Time management is essential here. The bigger picture is that you will have a number of assignments to complete, and probably domestic and other commitments as well. At the start of each semester, create a chart or diary of what needs to be handed in when, and factor in any other commitments.

You could combine this with the following breakdown of activities. This shows how to plan your work, from receiving an essay title at the start of term, to the hand-in date, usually 10–12 weeks later (sometimes longer, if holidays are included).

- Unpacking the assignment title.

- Relating information covered in teaching sessions to the title.

- Following up on reading set in lectures.

- Searching the Internet for information.

- Talking to the tutor about the assignment.

- Discussing ways of tackling the assignment with other students.

- Planning your assignment.

- Doing a first draft.

- Sharing your draft with a colleague and receiving feedback.

- Editing and proof-reading your second draft.

- Checking all references against departmental conventions/referencing guidelines.

UNPACKING THE ASSIGNMENT TITLE

Be very clear about what you're being asked to do, because planning your response to an assignment question starts here. This links back to getting to know what your tutor is really after and making sure you meet their particular requirements – explicit and implicit.

Worked example on children's rights

If the assignment title is 'It's all very well saying that you aim to do things in the child's best interests, until you come to put this into practice. Discuss, with reference to a particular context of your own choosing' on a module which has explored childhood and human rights, ask yourself what the tutor is *really* getting at.

CONTINUED

If, for example, the module has explored the tensions between different perspectives by asking you to debate tensions between protectionist as opposed to liberationist views of the child then the tutor is *really* asking you

- to theorize definitions/views of 'the child' and, hence, constructions of children's 'needs' and 'best interests'

- to explore how these might impact on different stakeholders' views of 'best interest'

- to identify and highlight the tensions and challenges of operationalizing policy (e.g. the UN convention).

They want you

- to show that you realize that 'it depends': that the tensions relate to who makes the decisions in relation to notions of inclusion and integration

- to unpack views, for and against, and compare and contrast them in a theorized and well-read manner

- to locate your discussion in a specific area/context, such as the smacking debate, children's clothes and uniforms, outdoor play or special education.

To build up a clear view of this, you should thoroughly work out how the teaching sessions relate to the title, look at the set reading, and talk to peers and tutors about the assignment. This will be done over several weeks, and emphasizes, once again, that you need to get to know your tutor via their lecturing and handouts, as well as from discussion with them.

Worked example on children's literature

The assignment title is: '"Filth, which ever way you look at it": discuss the depiction of teenage sexual activity in Burgess's (2003) controversial novel for young readers, *Doing It*.'

Here the tutor is *really* asking you

- about the different perspectives on the perceived value of children's books

- to provide an analysis of the *reasons* advocates of Burgess like his book, as opposed to the *reasons* opponents hold for disliking it.

They want you

- to draw on theoretical models from your secondary reading.

This example shows that reading/research for this title need not necessarily be about Burgess's book, but *should* be about theoretical writing which explains the different ways in which literature can be valued. Here wider reading helps create a framework for discussion and helps you articulate the issues that the essay title is getting at.

As the worked examples show, an effective assignment tends to draw, albeit implicitly, on a wide range of research. It also draws on your understanding of the concepts that inform the whole module, rather than 'just' material that directly relates to the specific topic that the essay title mentions.

WHAT IF YOU GET TO CHOOSE YOUR OWN TITLE?

Even if you have to respond to the same title as everyone else, there isn't one 'correct' answer, and you need your own 'angle' or focus. But sometimes you get to choose your focus entirely. If so, it is crucial to think about the learning outcomes, assessment criteria and what we said about 'getting to know your tutor' when deciding what to write about. For instance:

What if, in relation to the children's literature module above, instead of a specific title on Burgess' *Doing It*, the essay question was as follows?

'Write on a topic of your own choice related to the aims and learning outcomes of the module.'

What would help you choose something appropriate?

Read the module guide

In most cases the tutor will give some suggestions for topics to get students started and show the type of essay they are after. For this module the suggestions were:

- the presentation of a **problem, issue or theme** for contemporary children, such as the depiction of death, violence, family life, divorce, school, growing up, gender, class, race

- a particular **theoretical issue or debate**, such as the concept of bibliotherapy, censorship, the so-called 'new realism', the educational value of children's books, the ways in which books 'teach' (didacticism and the children's book)

- a particular **type** (genre) of children's book, such as the animal story, the futuristic novel, science fiction, fantasy, comedy, historical novels and so on.

Note and take account of any particular requirements

For this module, for instance, the tutor stipulated:

'Your assignment should review and evaluate **specific examples** of children's books in depth.'

This means that they want to see that you can *apply theoretical concepts*, ideas and frameworks to actual examples of children's books. You must, therefore, carefully choose those children's books if you want to do well.

● Reflect on the aims and learning outcomes

For this module the aims were

1   To provide an introduction to a range of modern children's authors and examples of their work.

2   To consider the **potential value** of the different literary experiences being created for children.

3   To identify and explore **the competing criteria** by which modern children's fiction may be **evaluated.**

The learning outcomes were that, after following this unit of study, students should be able to:

1   Identify, select and **contrast** a range of books written for children.

2   **Critically evaluate** the **potential value** of selected books for children and young people.

3   Demonstrate awareness of **the criteria** by which children's fiction may be judged and identify **their own criteria and framework** for making judgements.

These also give you a strong steer as to how to focus your assignment. They emphasize issues about the value of literature. They also flag up that perspectives on, and judgements of, children's fiction are important. In addition, the learning outcomes also emphasize that these issues should be discussed in relation to specific texts.

● Reflect on the assessment criteria

Although not always available, in this example these were:

WORKED EXAMPLE

Content

- Clearly stated purpose, identifying, selecting and analysing an appropriate range of books for children, rationalizing the choice.

- Feasible scope and focus.

- Sustained, thoroughly developed argument, based on high-level understanding.

- Evidence of close reading of primary texts and use of relevant ideas from secondary theoretical literature.

- Evidence of appreciation, insight and understanding of key relevant issues, ideas and theories relating to the course.

- Evidence of awareness of relevant debates and dilemmas that surround the production and evaluation of texts for an intended child audience.

Structure

- Logical order, with clear signposts to let the reader know where the ideas are going and why they are important.

Style and presentation

- Appropriate academic style, with accurate referencing following departmental conventions.

- Grammar, spelling, vocabulary appropriate to selected topic.

This sets out, very clearly, the possibilities and limits for your choice of essay title and offers clues on how to go about writing the assignment. It emphasizes the need to apply theory from the secondary reading to primary texts, for instance, and reinforces the module aims.

In effect, the module guide gives you part of the recipe for successful assignment writing.

Now compare the way in which two students approached this assignment.

Student 1

The first student decided to write **'An exploratory study of teenage problem fiction'.**

This outlined the range of problems that can be tackled in modern children's fiction for teenagers, including drugs, sex, pregnancy, alcohol, homelessness, growing up and puberty, divorce and identity formation.

The student explained how lots of books were written for teenagers designed to tackle these issues and problems, and summarized the plots of several, including two Judy Blume titles, one novel on teenage pregnancy written in the 1960s, one book on bullying, one high fantasy and one book from the 1990s on teenage relationships.

The student found an article saying that teenage years were stressful and that children needed books that helped them cope with the stresses of adolescent life. The introduction to the assignment cited this article, and a range of very generalized secondary literature which said that teenage fiction was an important and growing genre with a long history.

Finally, the student compared and contrasted the chosen books' approaches by pointing out that some used fantasy and some used realism to help teenagers come to terms with the problems they often face.

Tutor comments

- The assignment covered too much material and was not sufficiently focused.

- There was little awareness of the relativity of the many 'problems' discussed.

- While there was evidence of some wider reading it was very general and the student was uncritical of authorities (accepting, rather than questioning, comments about whether books help children overcome problems).

- The student did not think critically about the implication that child readers get and accept a single message from any given book.

CONTINUED

To summarize, the student did not perceive issues around the critical reception of books, nor the qualitative differences between the books' approaches to the problems they raised. The student earned a low 2:2. While they were hardworking, they were insufficiently tuned in to the key concepts and debates of the module.

Student 2

The second student took a very different approach.

'An exploration of the critical reception of the work of illustrator Roberto Innocenti: the challenges of illustrating the Holocaust for young readers.'

This focused on Roberto Innocenti's illustrations, predominantly in *Rose Blanche* (2003) but also Vander See's *Erika's Story* (2003). The assignment cited an article in *The Times* that questioned the suitability of these books for young readers, arguing that they would be 'puzzled' by the works. The student argued that Innocenti's pictures encourage a reader's questions and that he seeks to broaden the reader's understanding through this process of individual discovery.

The student also addressed questions raised by the review regarding the morality of exposing children to the Holocaust and responded to this by presenting the dangers of assuming that a child has no knowledge of suffering, in addition arguing that the emotions (fear, prejudice, anger, isolation) are feelings contemporary children share and experience in their own lives.

The student also drew on theory, particularly in analysing how Innocenti seeks to inspire connections between the protagonists through the concept of 'bridging metaphors' (Davies, 2000), which, thinking laterally, she drew from reading about citizenship education (as opposed to children's literature criticism).

CONTINUED

Tutor comments

- This assignment was tightly focused and showed a clear engagement with the texts.

- The student had thought critically about authorities and critiqued their take on the way that children understand and interpret texts.

- An engagement had been made with the ways in which children's literature is evaluated.

- The student had drawn on a range of critical literature, applying it well to the examples chosen.

The student earned a First having tuned in to the module's concerns effectively.

Now let's turn to compare different aspects of these two essays to clarify how, from them, you can learn how to produce a good, focused assignment.

Titles

The title is very important. It steers the reader, ensuring that they understand what the assignment is about from the start. The first title is too broad, while the second is tightly focused and descriptive of the subject.

Arguments

In the first assignment, the argument is 'problem books help children'. This is too simplistic, and doesn't take account of other theoretical perspectives – it sees 'problem literature' as straightforward and 'problems' as uncontested. The student has just 'put in' irrelevant secondary reading on the history of teenage literature, rather than using her reading to construct a case and make relevant points. It is all about gathering information, not analysis. In contrast, the second essay appreciates complexity, arguing that Innocenti's work, while it has been seen by critics as problematic in relation to a child audience, can also be seen as an important route into exploring historical events. Further, she argues that the critics reveal the limits of their perception of children's literature and children through their comments about the books. There is an appreciation of possible meanings, values and judgements about children's literature, and various constructions of childhood, embedded within the argument.

'Plans' or spider diagrams

When the student drew the plan for the first essay it had 'TEENAGE PROBLEMS TACKLED' at its centre. 'Theory' only occupied one offshoot box (and was very limited, at that). Any other offshoot boxes had the titles of primary texts in them. It was, bluntly, too broad, unfocused and woolly, and she never refined her original working title. In comparison, the second plan had 'OBJECTIONS TO DEPICTION OF HOLOCAUST FOR CHILDREN' in the centre (note that this was an *issue*, which helped to strengthen the essay). The student used this as a working title, refining it as she went along, until it got sharper and sharper. She made sure her sharpest was the one she submitted. Other offshoot boxes had theoretical perspectives in them on, firstly, images, then reader response and multivalent texts, irony and, finally, secondary literature from liberationist perspectives (children have a right to know and be informed *or* children already live in world of violence/experience) versus protectionist ones (children should be kept in innocence), views which related to literature about constructions of the child such as James and Prout (1997). Further, there were boxes about children's rights debates and on teaching about the Holocaust (such as the writing by Davies). Finally, there were boxes focusing on analysing children's books in terms of, for example, the use of ending, the image of the child, the depiction of 'evil' and use to which it is put. These boxes all became key subheadings in her assignment.

Use of reading

The first student shows a limited awareness of a (one-sided) literature. The second student shows a higher understanding due to their wider reading and awareness of issues and concepts. She has grasped that criteria for evaluation are problematical and contested (something which the learning outcomes refer to). The writing draws on a wide range of literatures and applies them appropriately.

TACKLING OTHER TYPES OF ASSIGNMENT

You are likely to be faced with a range of assessment strategies on your CS/ECS course. However, essay/assignment writing still tends to be the predominant form of assessment. There are many variations, but they all demand approaches to preparation similar to that for an essay.

For all the following, the basic rule is to check that you 'know your tutor' and seek out the assessment criteria.

Portfolios are becoming a common form of assessment. It is tempting to accumulate quantity instead of quality, but don't just hurl a load of material in. Tutors will want to see 'evidence' of your achievement in relation to specific learning outcomes. It's sensible to place your evidence (a lesson plan, an extract from a research diary you kept during a child observation or placement, an example of children's drawings, an annotated bibliography of reading or whatever else you've done during the module) into appendices and cross-reference these to

a) a contents page (closely tied to the specified learning outcomes and/or assessment criteria)

b) a discussion which highlights what you have learned, and draws attention to the evidence that can be found in your appendices.

The important thing is to help the reader find their way around your portfolio, rather than making them wade through lots of material.

Annotated bibliographies are set to encourage you to précis and summarize a wide range of sources, and test your skills of synthesis, comparison and contrast of theoretical perspectives. Make sure, then, that you *say something* and make points about the reading you conduct (you are often asked to 'critically analyse' it), rather than simply report it. Draw out similarities, differences and key perspectives.

Exams can be of several kinds. If the paper is seen in advance, then prepare as you would for an essay, but then, basically, learn that essay before you go into the exam hall.

If it is an unseen paper, then you should see what past papers are available (to get a sense of the kind of questions asked), read through the module guide, especially the assessment criteria, and set yourself to memorizing material on the subject. You have been reading around, and what you know from that reading will make your answers richer.

Remember it isn't facts that are usually being sought, but an argument, just like the essay, which draws on your secondary reading and your grasp of the issues. It is too easy, in exams, to write down everything you know about a subject rather than be selective and really answer the questions. Take a little time, after you have turned the paper over, to make sure that you have interpreted the question correctly, unpacking it as you would an essay question, rather than rushing into writing.

Presentations You may be asked to do these on your own or as part of a team. Again, make sure you know what, precisely, you are to present on, and prepare accordingly. Many students slip into thinking that pre-sentations 'simply' test their presentation skills – whether they speak clearly, make eye contact with the audience, invite questions, have good visual aids and handouts, use PowerPoint and IT effectively and so on. This is, indeed, one aspect of presentations, and might be the main rea-son a lecturer uses it, especially in the early stages of your course.

On the other hand, though, most of the marks might actually be awarded for content – the sorts of things demanded in assignment writing – so check the assessment criteria. A presentation on the subject 'Show aware-ness of the implications of adult perceptions of risk on children's out-door play', for instance, is clearly interested in the substantive topic area and research, not presentation skills. As we emphasized above, your assignment can look great, but if it doesn't have a well-developed focus and argument then it won't do very well and the same is true of presen-tations.

Reflective commentaries These are increasingly being set in order to encourage self- and peer-review skills – and to reward the vital key skills that you'll need to do well in your studies and when you graduate. Again, make sure you know what they're after, and don't assume that they're asking for personal, opinionated writing. Lecturers will be looking for theorized thoughts that show what you have learned.

What is the focus of my reflective commentary supposed to be?

You might be asked to evaluate your own learning progress as part of a portfolio of evidence in the initial stages of your course. You can't just write 'I got much better'. Instead look at what lecturers want you to get better in. Imagine the learning outcomes and criteria ask that you 'Appreciate that competing images and ideologies of childhood exist'. In response you could include, as an appendix, your summaries of different secondary reading you have done. In your reflective commentary you could draw out the different perspectives, highlighting their similarities and differences in relation to the views of childhood.

Another example might be a reflective commentary focused on getting better at writing about childhood and using theory, like the writing tasks on social construction we showed you in the last chapter. You could include, as an appendix, an early stab you made at writing a response on the early stages of your course (as seen in Chapter 3). A good reflective commentary would look at the strengths and weaknesses of that piece of writing and would suggest what you would do to improve in future. You could include a redrafted piece of writing as another appendix.

Design, project or problem-based/enquiry-based activities Sometimes you will be asked to apply your knowledge to a 'real world' issue, challenge or problem. An example might be 'Design a drugs awareness programme for teenagers, and theorize your response.' If you're asked to theorize or draw upon literature, you should offer your outline, but also discuss possible alternatives, showing *how* and *why* you have designed the programme the way you have.

DISSERTATIONS OR INDEPENDENT PROJECTS

Doing a good dissertation

An independent project or dissertation is a typical assessment in the final year of any CS/ECS Honours degree. This usually involves collecting some 'real world' data, gathering information on the views, opinions and perspectives of stakeholders, such as parents, teachers, police, medics, children, librarians, health visitors, nursery officers, or exploring dimensions of practice, such as work with children in classrooms, retail, looked after children, social services, respite services, youth services. You'll usually be expected to use research methods such as interviews, participant observation, research diaries or questionnaire surveys.

This may sound daunting, as do the words 'doing research'. Some people panic at this point and forget what they know about writing good assignments, which is a shame as doing a dissertation or project is very similar.

The size of the project, as it can typically be 9–12,000 words long, may also create panic and cause students to choose a topic that is too big. However, once students get into writing their dissertation they always say it's far too *few* words to say what they want to say and their advice to you is to *focus on a sharper topic*. You have been doing shorter pieces of writing that follow the same rule for several years by now, so don't be panicked by the larger scale.

In effect, what makes a good assignment also makes a good dissertation or project. General principles apply: just as you need an 'angle' in your assignments, based on theoretical explorations of debates and issues, so you need one for a dissertation. A research question will, as in an essay, often start by looking for varying perspectives, and the reasons people hold those views.

Make sure you focus and choose a feasible topic

The key to success is choosing a good research question. Build in time for this as it can take a while. For example:

A student became interested in the issue of how few men there seemed to be in the childcare settings she'd visited. She knew this was a topical issue, and that there was debate about how difficult it was to attract men to childcare roles, and, further, that opinion was divided about whether it was deemed 'a good thing' to recruit men to work in nurseries. On the one hand, men could be seen as positive role models for children by, for instance, challenging stereotypes of men as uncaring, but on the other hand, she knew male carers met with resistance and suspicion.

This was still, however, too big a focus. One way to narrow her gaze was to think about whose views she might want to research. She could have looked at employers' perspectives on the challenges and issues surrounding men in childcare, or she could have looked at parents' perspectives, or other (female) nursery officers' views.

This student chose, however, to explore the views of male nursery officers themselves. She identified and interviewed male nursery officers in her region and compared and contrasted their views about being in this role, about other people's perceptions of them, about what drew them to the profession, about barriers and rewards – in sum, how they felt about themselves in relation to their professional identity as a man in a female-dominated profession. This meant her project started to focus on questions of personal identity and she became immersed in the literature on identity and construction of self.

Depending on the research question she could also have taken the literature search in other directions, for example into literature on masculinities, or on managing people. In effect, there is no 'correct' literature, just a huge range of potential sources of ideas and concepts.

Another student wanted to teach and specialize in English. She knew, therefore, that she wanted to focus on the National Literacy Strategy for her dissertation.

CONTINUED

Again, she had to focus down, and decided to look particularly at the issue of shared reading. Her inspiration was observing teachers deliver the literacy hour and noticing the differences in their use of shared reading. Her literature search revealed different perspectives on the value and purpose of reading – from Cooling (1998) and Dombey (2000) who valued imagination, promotion and a whole-book approach, to a very different view based around skills development.

The student had also noticed that not all teachers used story-time, and decided to see, when they did, how their views of its value compared and contrasted. Her dissertation became about teachers' views of delivering literacy via shared reading and she interviewed two experienced and two newly qualified teachers as part of her research.

Let's look at the second study in more detail, to illuminate some other related areas of doing well in dissertations.

REPORTING THE DATA YOU COLLECT EFFECTIVELY

Most dissertation assessment criteria (and, incidentally, any other more 'practical' or research-led reports or fieldwork-based assignments you might be required to do on CS/ECS courses) focus on your data analysis skills.

The student eventually reported her findings under subheadings, which she established by looking for key themes and issues in the interview data.

The subheadings she used were:

1 Teachers' concerns about the National Literacy Strategy

All four teachers mentioned the fast pace of the National Literacy Strategy and expressed concerns about differentiating the curriculum for children with special educational needs. However, there were marked differences, which formed the basis for the next subheadings.

CONTINUED

2   Teachers' views of the value of the National Literacy Strategy

Experienced teachers were annoyed by it and found it intrusive and prescriptive. Newly qualified teachers expressed no concerns. The student backed up this general point by quoting a teacher as an illustration: *'The children keep stopping to focus on capital letters and full stops: they'll even shout out every time they see a capital letter! But reading should be enjoyable, not reduced to being treated like a quiz or a puzzle'.*

3   Teachers' views of the autonomous learner

The student noted marked differences in the levels of responsibility teachers expected or demanded of the children. She talked about how often experienced teachers used words like 'independently' and encouraged the children to 'join in'. New teachers, by contrast, seemed to have a view of passive children: *'I like the children to sit on the carpet and for me to teach the skills. I can keep track of the objectives I'm teaching this way.'*

4   Motivation

Experienced teachers believed children were motivated by reading whole books, making comments like *'Story-time is good because it opens up discussion'* (using the term 'opens up' also suggests this teacher values children having a say or an opinion). These teachers also valued fun: *'I love to see the excitement on their faces during story-time.'*

New teachers, in comparison, used reward systems to motivate – giving out stickers and stamps for *'working hard'*: *'I don't stop and discuss the pictures. One main reason for having story-time is to help develop their listening skills, as they have really bad listening skills.'*

Instead of simply reporting what the teachers said, the student concentrated on making points about the teachers' views. For example, she wrote

One possible interpretation is that because the newly qualified teachers appeared to view the learner in a passive role, then they felt that it is their duty

to be teaching the learner some sort of skill. During story-time it is listening skills

It is important to note that key themes are not 'fixed'. They depend on your 'angle', your research question and design of the research instruments (the ways of collecting data, devising interview schedules and so on) and your awareness and 'take' on the reading you have done.

So, then, how did this student pull out these themes and produce such a good dissertation? First she chose a **research question** that looked for different perspectives, based on contrasting stakeholders' views, and she explored how these views compared to the theories (perceptions of value) she'd read about.

When she came to gather and subsequently report her data, she collected and analysed it systematically, informed by her reading and understanding of the topic area. This gave her key headings to work with. She got them by a process of

a) summarizing each interviewee's viewpoint (known as data reduction) – précising their views by condensing them onto separate sheets of paper (one per teacher)

b) comparing and contrasting the sheets of paper, deliberately looking for similarities and differences between the teachers' views. To do this she picked out the main themes and issues, then set about coding everything each teacher said by asking key questions of the data

    – trying to assess the strength of support for particular views

    – looking for opinions for or against

    – looking for any gaps or surprising omissions (things they might have been expected to say), which implies she had read around the issues *before* starting her research.

This process allowed her to go through all the interview transcripts (raw data) in a systematic way, coding bits of text by using different coloured highlighter pens. This gave her a framework for discussing her findings. These were then related to the literature search chapter, and she had identified illustrative quotes from the interviewees to include as evidence in her report, as we discussed above.

DATA ANALYSIS AND CODING

The following example shows what we mean by this in a little more detail. Here are a number of extracts from interviews with different parents about their views of the purposes of outdoor play.

1

I don't know, I mean, you hear so much about kids having accidents when they play out. They're bad enough when you've got them with you; I know our Carl's always hurting hisself even when he's just in the garden at home. And that's when there's just him and me with him all the time. So, well, I don't know, I like to think he's in the house and I know where he is.

2

Well, my lot just love being outdoors. They come in filthy mind you, but, well, you can't really enjoy yourself and not get mucky when you're that age, can you? I remember when me and Pete, my brother, we used to nip off down the rec, like a big park with woods and that near our place, and we used to get up to all sorts. Course, nowadays you'd be worried for strangers and perverts, but then we used to just play and build dens and make up stories and it was our special place. No grown ups. Just us. That's what we liked, being able to do our own thing and no one telling us not.

3

You mean, if they were at nursery and they were just playing out all day? I'm not sure about that at all. I mean, what do you send them to school for if they're just doing stuff they could do at home anyway? I mean, they've got time enough to play out on the weekends and heaven knows. They've got precious little time to learn all the stuff they need to get through before they're getting sorted into sets for Maths and sets for

English. And my two, well, it's hard enough to get them to sit down and concentrate on anything for more than 30 seconds as it is. They'd like nothing better than to be up and out rolling in the mud all day and building dens and the like. But that's not going to be much good to them when they leave school is it? You don't see many jobs with 'hut building' in them! No, if Mrs T at the nursery started on that lark I'd be thinking about moving my boys.

4

For me, it's about giving them a chance to have a bit of freedom for once. Kids nowadays, they seem to be always being bombarded by what they're meant to be doing, not what they want to do. I don't agree with that. It puts pressure on parents to hear their reading. It's like you're a bad mother if you just have a romp. Last Sunday we all went down to the Dene and hunted for conkers. I used to love that when I was a kid. And Terry, he was really good at it. He kept thinking of ways to get them down, out of the trees and he made up this game where he was a squirrel and we all had to chase him and try and find his secret hoard. And at the end, I don't know, we just seemed to be closer, much closer than if we'd spent the morning doing homework or something. And on the way back we stopped off at his gran's and she dug out some pictures of me when I was his age and she reminded us of how me and our Lynne used to meet up with the kids along the way and built a bogey, you know, a cart sort of thing, and used to give each other rides. I'd forgotten till she reminded us, but it was really good. In fact, I've probably forgotten half the stuff I did when I was a kid, but that just brought back so many memories, you know: of being young and having fun, and secrets, and I suppose that's the kind of memories I want my kids to have. Not all school and studying and doing worksheets. More about having fun and feeling you're more . . . not just always doing what your mum or your teacher tells you.

5

You worry though, don't you? I mean about what people will say about you if they see your kids outside, especially at night or if it's dark early. It's just there's so much nowadays about stranger danger – you can hardly open the paper without reading about some kid that's been abused. And we don't even know half the time that there's blokes with records for that sort of thing living in the area. As a parent you just can't be too careful. You've got to look after them. I'd never ever forgive myself if anything happened to any of my kids.

6

I suppose I'd be a bit worried about what they'd be getting up to. I mean, you know what they're like in the playground, that's when all the trouble seems to happen. And it might sound all very nice: freedom, exploring, playing and stuff, but my little girl, well she's quite nervous you know. And some of the lads in that nursery they can be quite naughty and rough and they're quite a handful to the teacher even when they're in the class. So I'm not sure that I'd be certain my daughter would be really safe if they were running around all over the place and not being like closely supervised you know.

For the first step (data reduction) you could briefly summarize each one's viewpoint, with a bullet point giving a brief overview of what each is saying about children playing outdoors. You could then move your analysis further by highlighting those 'for' and 'against': parents 2 and 4 are for outdoor play, while 1, 3, 5 and 6 are against it.

Next, having looked at the data, think of possible categories/subheadings to report your work under. This helps you engage with the possible reasons why parents hold their views, and focuses you on the differences, as well as the similarities.

For	Against
Views of children's independence, autonomy and choice	Risk and adult protectionism (i.e. independence seen as threatening)
Skills development	Perceptions of time wasted
Children need freedom to explore	Children need protection/teaching by adults. Perceptions of risk
Good parents enable	Fears of being labelled 'bad' parent
Romantic views of the child	Fears of children as violent or aggressive

These broad categories are not end of the story, however, but can serve to get you started. Like our previous student you could use quotations from the data to show that the picture is more complex again, reading further into interviewees' perspectives – just like we said about reading into and analysing secondary texts. What's important is that you begin to see there's a lot to be said about your data, so that you focus down in a sharper way, if you need to. Too many students don't make the most of their research when it comes to writing it up, because they haven't sufficiently analysed it and don't include illustrative quotations.

For example, some parents shared a concern about a particular issue, but for different reasons. Both 6 and 5 offered comments that fall under the subheading 'Children need protection'. However, 6 is concerned about protecting her child from other children: ' . . . I'm not sure that I'd be certain my daughter would be really safe if they [the lads] were running around all over the place and not being like closely supervised . . . ' In addition, in citing boys as the problem, she is flagging up gender issues around outdoor play. In contrast, parent 5 sees other adults as the issue: 'It's just there's so much nowadays about stranger danger – you can hardly open the paper without reading about some kid that's been abused', a very different view of what is ostensibly the same issue.

Similarly, you could imagine a subheading on views of the child. Views were often underpinned by varying notions about 'proper' childhood.

Some parents saw the child as inherently independent and appeared to subscribe to Romantic views of the child. One, for example, held the view that outdoor play was a valuable way to share family heritage and stimulate emotional development, saying: *'For me, it's about giving them a chance to have a bit of freedom for once'*. Further, 4 argued that outdoor play *'brought back so many memories, you know: of being young and having fun, and secrets, and I suppose that's the kind of memories I want my kids to have'*.

Another subheading or theme could surround views of adult roles and responsibilities. Here you could discuss interviewees' perceptions that were related to views of the role of parents as protectors/policing and ensuring safety. As 1 said, *' . . . I like to think he's in the house and I know where he is'*. Other points you could make when unpacking the data could relate to views of the role of adults as educators and the view that outdoor play is perceived as time wasting. As 3 argued, *'But that's not going to be much good to them when they leave school is it? You don't see many jobs with "hut building" in them!'* Others seemed worried about being labelled an irresponsible parent. As 5 said, *'I mean about what people will say about you if they see your kids outside, especially at night or if it's dark early'*.

AND FINALLY . . . USING FEEDBACK

It's vital to use and reflect on feedback – but tutors can use strange language, so you need to know how to translate it and, even more importantly, apply it as advice for the next assignment, as it is often generic and so applicable to more than one piece of work. Don't think 'I've done that one now, forget it and move on' – learn from feedback.

What tutors mean

These examples offer 'plain English' interpretations of tutor comments and what students could do in response to particular feedback.

Tutor comment: 'Your essay is strong on personal opinion'.

What this actually means is: You must learn to qualify statements.

What you could do to improve might include:

- analysing what the essay is asking you to do from the start

- using quotations to illustrate points

- further reading around the literature to uncover the range of perspectives on the issue

- citation of other people's views on the issue

- using wider reading to locate and back up different perspectives

- analysis of other people's perspectives

- comparing and contrasting other people's perspectives in the literature

- helping your reader locate any literature they may be interested in reading.

Tutor comment: 'You must learn to reference correctly'.

What this actually means is: You are not following the Harvard System, either within the body of the essay and/or in the reference list at the end.

What you could do to improve might include:

- evidencing all statements with authoritative comments based on recognized academic literature

- being cautious about the authority of material you get from the Web

- using a guide to the Harvard referencing system.

This will help because

- the reader of your essay can see where your ideas have come from

- it helps you avoid plagiarism.

CONTINUED

Tutor comment: 'Your essay is difficult to follow'.

What this actually means is: The argument is disjointed, does not follow a logical sequence, jumps from important to unimportant points randomly. There is no direction to the essay and it may even contradict itself.

What you could do to improve might include:

- planning your essay
- structuring it in paragraphs
- using subheadings
- proof-reading
- thinking about what the title is asking you to do
- sticking to the point
- working out your argument/establishing a central thesis statement
- asking someone to read the essay, for spelling and grammatical errors.

It is also very important to understand feedback if you have to do re-sits – use it to help you prepare.

Peer- and self-review as a source of feedback

It is not just written tutor comments on your work that constitutes feedback, but a range of information, including comments from peers and self-reflection.

Talking to tutors and fellow students (both in your current year group and the years ahead) can help you to clarify your own ideas. The 'not knowing what I think till I hear what I say' phenomenon emphasizes the importance of rehearsing and trying out your ideas in oral presentations, however informal.

Here's a student talking about how imperative it is to get used to working with others.

I like working with other people, and although it's a bit funny other people seeing your work, I've got used to it. Getting to know people in the tutorials has meant you feel OK about saying: 'Oh, I did it this way. How did you do yours?' And then you get the opinions of the whole group, not just your own ideas. So that's got to be better than doing it on your own. And you learn from making mistakes.

The following student comment also highlights how valuable it is to share your ideas and get feedback on how others are approaching an assignment. This is not a case of copying, but of getting useful alternative strategies for tackling assignments. This student has learned the need to focus from peers and concrete examples, as well as from tutors.

One of my [core module] essays was on child development. At first I was doing it overall, and it was quite hard, trying to cover everything, and do it justice, because I'd done a plan of all the aspects, and I chose the main ones we'd covered all through the semester. After I went to the tutorial [where group menbers discussed their essay plans], though, I saw it'd make more sense to choose one specific area of development, and really go for that. Because looking at the development of pre-school children is so vast. So listening to other people, not so much tutors, but people on my level, really helped.

So, the final advice of this chapter is to start early, manage your time effectively, and build incrementally in writing assignments of any kind. Further, ask if you are not sure about anything and seek feedback on your interpretation of what is expected. Finally, revisit your work and check you're on the right lines by running ideas past peers and lecturers.

Chapter 5

Getting a Job

This chapter will explore a range of directions that you might consider taking after leaving university. It covers the following topics:

- Where do I go from here?

- Applying for jobs and courses

- Interviews

WHERE DO I GO FROM HERE?

Graduating and starting a career is rarely the first thing anyone thinks about when they initially arrive at university. Getting to grips with the university experience is challenging and exciting enough. However, this chapter gives some pointers about what you might want to do next and how you can prepare yourself for future employment.

Some people do have a specific career in mind when they begin their studies, but it is more likely that you will use the time you spend at university to explore possibilities, particularly through placements, if they are part of your degree. In addition, ask yourself, 'Where do I want to be in five years time?' You might also like to reflect on which modules you have enjoyed the most as you go through your degree, as they are going to point to careers that you would, ideally, like to enter.

You may also change your mind about where you want to go after graduation, given the range of possibilities that these subject areas can open up. These are comparatively new subject areas and no one has yet worked out the full range of possible careers to which they might lead.

What jobs are there?

- Working with children, via careers such as teaching.

- Working for children, as in Early Years and other settings.

- Postgraduate research and other further study.

- Careers that don't involve working with children or young people. Many employers do not look for specific degree subjects, so you do need to be able to discuss your own work in relation to what they are looking for.

- Possible career areas in relation to the first two options include: education, playwork, social care, librarianship, child psychology, children's rights, Sure Start, health, reader development, the voluntary sector (from large charities such as NCH or Barnardos to smaller local organizations).

Equally, you may discover as your studies continue that you want to develop your research skills further through postgraduate study, in the form of an MA or MSc, having become interested in specific aspects of the degree you have taken. You may also take further qualifications that lead into specific careers, such as PGCE, QTS or Social Work certificates.

Applying for . . .

MA/MSc (Master of Arts/Master of Science)

There are a number of ways to approach this. Doing a search via Google on a subject area, say play, and combining that word with MA and UK, leads to a range of courses in that area.

Alternatively, if your study keeps mentioning specific researchers whose work interests you, find out where they are based and look at the courses offered by their institution.

CONTINUED

University websites are always going to be the best place to gather information on postgraduate courses. These same sites will also have copies of the relevant forms, and give contacts for a team who field enquiries. There should also be information about funding for both part-time and full-time courses.

PGCE (Postgraduate Certificate in Education)

The PGCE is the most popular route into teaching for new graduates. Apply via the Graduate Teacher Training Registry (GTTR) at www.gttr.ac.uk. The initial closing date is around the 15th December although some courses may have places after this date. Applications can be made online and are processed as soon as they are received so it is wise to act early.

Primary courses fill quickly, but secondary PGCE places are less competitive so there isn't quite the urgency to make an early application.

With regard to secondary PGCE places, in order to teach in secondary schools applicants need to show good subject knowledge related to their named subject specialism.

SCITT (School Centred Initial Teacher Training)

These programmes are a realistic alternative to the PGCE. SCITTs are provided by a consortium of schools or by LEAs and are usually affiliated to a university. Training is more school-based as the title suggests. Application is through the GTTR or in some cases directly to the SCITT itself. Your application will not be considered if you do not show that you have some recent experience in a school or other learning setting.

Both programmes of training lead to QTS (Qualified Teacher Status). Both the PGCE and SCITT offer similar employment prospects and, at the time of writing, have the same training bursary. For more information the Teacher Training Agency (TTA) website is a good starting point. Their helpline is 0845 6000991 or you can contact them via www.canteach.gov.uk.

CONTINUED

GTP (Graduate Teacher Programme)

This is the employment-based route that was originally introduced to address the problem of filling teacher vacancies in certain subject and geographical areas. Unqualified teachers are employed by and trained in a specific school, gaining QTS this way. The scheme was introduced to attract mature entrants or those who may already be working in a school. Entry is now open to all ages. However, the proportion of places in relation to other routes is still relatively small so applicants who have built up a wide range of experiences are preferred. This doesn't mean to say it is not a viable option for anyone who may need to earn a salary while training. For the up-to-date situation locally contact the TTA helpline (see above).

Alternatively, the skills that studying has given you, irrespective of subject, are going to be useful to employers, and you may want to look at going into a career which doesn't involve working with or for children or young people.

In all of these cases you will need to write applications and be interviewed, so elements in this chapter address these topics. These aspects of the chapter might also help you with any job applications you make while at university.

APPLYING FOR JOBS AND COURSES

Keep records

Get organized now. Create a file that contains all your certificates and professional documents alongside other important material such as copies of driving licences, passport details and your National Insurance Number.

In addition, a 'career file' can also contain letters of support or references you have received, either from school, college or employers, whether part or full time. This will remind you of the different jobs you have had when creating a CV, but will also act as a list of potential referees when you are writing applications.

⬤ Write your CV

A CV needs to detail your education, qualifications and employment history. The careers department in your university will be able to help you to create one, but the following offers a brief guide of what to include. You can use this either to apply for jobs (if the employer asks for a CV), or as a reminder of what you have done when filling in application forms.

Curriculum Vitae

Name

Address

Telephone	Include your mobile number
Education	Include dates of study and the name and address of the institutions involved
Qualifications	Include level and grade
In-service Training	If applicable
Employment	Start with your most recent, or current, post and work backwards. Include the employer's name and address, your dates of employment, the post you held, and finally the main responsibilities you fulfilled.
Other Interests	It is not just your professional or academic qualifications that employers are interested in, but also your breadth of experience, from voluntary work to involvement in university societies and sports.

Finally, if there are any 'gaps' (time seen by employers as having been spent out of employment, such as when having a family or travelling abroad) make sure you include details, as employers will probably ask about these on interview.

The main body of application forms and covering letters

As we suggest above, you can apply in a number of different ways for jobs. Most now require you to fill in a form (and we cover that in a later section of this chapter). Others ask for a CV as we show above.

In addition, when sending a CV, you will sometimes need to send a covering letter. See this as a mini job application form. Figure 5.1 gives an idea of how to lay one out and what to say.

Combined with the information on the CV it will also give you the information you need to fill in most job application forms and Figure 5.1 gives an idea of the kind of language you can use when applying for posts. Use the framework it offers, but leave out the elements (e.g. address) that make it a letter.

The following sections (particularly that on 'The person specification') will help you to draft an effective covering letter and to fill in an application form, as both need to cover the main criteria that the employer is looking for.

Jobs and where to find them

There are many places where jobs are advertised and sifting through them to find relevant posts can be a huge task, so start exploring sources and sites now to get familiar with the field. However, don't let it get in the way of your studies. Be aware of key posts or graduate training schemes that you are interested in by your final year, but initially apply only for key schemes (the rest can wait until you have handed in the last piece of work). The final year of university involves a huge amount of work and so does making job applications. The latter should not be allowed to undermine the former.

Address
Telephone numbers
Date

Dear (insert contact name, or 'Sir/Madam'),

I am writing to apply for the post of (......) as advertised in (......). Having just completed my degree in Childhood Studies/Early Childhood Studies I am aiming to pursue a career in (......). I feel this position would provide me with valuable experience for my career progression.

My work in (......) for (give the period of time) has greatly increased my awareness of the importance of (......) and I have often found myself in a position of responsibility for (......). In such a varied role it is imperative that I take on a flexible approach to my work and manage my time well to meet deadlines.

My degree has supplemented and built on this knowledge as I have carried out research in areas such as (......). All of these studies have focused on (......) and I therefore have knowledge of some of the issues and problems that can arise.

Both my studies and employment have increased my interest in the areas of (......) and spurred my ambition to (......).

I always take on a positive approach to challenges I face in both my working and personal life. I expect this role will be demanding and I would enjoy using the skills I have acquired, both through my work and my studies.

Yours sincerely (or 'Yours faithfully' if you started with 'Dear Sir/Madam),

(Name)

Figure 5.1 Sample covering letter

There are a number of general websites, for instance www.prospects.ac.uk and www.milkround.co.uk, both of which offer advice to students and graduates and advertise job vacancies aimed at this group. Prospects, in particular, helps you to focus on areas of interest, offering descriptions of the jobs, case studies of people in those jobs and information about how to get into these areas.

In addition, university careers staff should be able to point you in the direction of other resources that might be useful. You can also discuss your likes and dislikes with them. This too can help focus your search. Job-hunting often seems straightforward until you set out on it, when the wealth of information can make you feel swamped. However, there is support available. You are not on your own.

If you have a specific career trajectory in mind there are more specific sources of information. For instance, if you want to work in social care then the *Guardian* on a Wednesday is essential reading. In contrast, prospective teachers should consider *The Times Educational Supplement* their key journal. If you want to work for a local authority, study their web pages as they usually contain job sections. Similarly, with regard to the voluntary sector, look at the websites of specific organizations.

Finding out about specific employers

Researching an organization will help you to assess whether you want to work in it, and help you to tailor your CV or job application. You can do this by using the Internet or writing to organizations directly for leaflets and brochures.

You not only want to find out about the history of the organization but also about how they are organized. For instance, are they local, regional or national in scope? Do they employ people from a range of professions or are they focused specifically on one area?

You also need to find out about the working arrangements such as flexi-time, holiday entitlement and whether you would be expected to work at weekends. Do they offer childcare support, opportunities to travel, and possibilities for promotion? What kind of salaries do they offer? How do they compare to other employers?

Even if it is early in your degree, you can send for details of jobs that you think look like something you might want to do in future. The pack you receive will contain not only details of the job itself but also background information on the organization and the person specification.

The person specification

The person specification can be really useful to you, as it is where the employer describes the *essential* and *desirable* criteria for the job. Every application will be assessed against these criteria and it is this process that creates the shortlist of people who will be interviewed. This is very much like writing an essay. Your tutors will have stressed that you must look at the marking criteria in order to check that you have covered all the aspects that the person marking the assignment is looking for. You must learn to present your experiences in ways that demonstrate that you meet these work-based specifications, just as you got to grips with those addressing assessed work.

This is just as important if you are applying for further training, as it is likely that the person specification will include something like, in the case of teacher training, 'direct experience of work in schools' or 'direct experience of work with children of a relevant age group'. The person specification tells you what experience you must build up if you are to be shortlisted for courses or jobs. There is little point, then, in applying for jobs for which you do not hold the essential criteria. For very popular jobs there may be many people who have the essential criteria and con-sequently those doing the shortlisting move to the desirable criteria as a way of sifting candidates. Make sure you also consider the desirable cri-teria and develop your skills and your experiences in these areas too.

Person specifications will also detail the qualifications necessary for the post. This helps you assess whether the jobs you are looking at match your capabilities. If the job asks for GCSE rather than degree qualifica-tions then you might feel frustrated or bored, although it might still offer useful experience (you may also be willing to take a job which is less well paid because you can see this as helping you to move on in your career). Bear in mind, however, that you could well be seen as over-qualified. Alternatively, if you feel that you are under-qualified for the posts that you are looking at then you might have actually identified not your first post, but one that you might like to move on to, in effect mapping out your career path.

Application forms

Most jobs now require you to fill in, and either post or deliver by hand, an application form that asks for details of your education, employment and experiences (just like a CV, but in their chosen format). As the only information that people will have about you is what you put in this application form it is important for it to be legible, free of spelling mistakes or typos, and showing your skills and experience as effectively as possible. In addition, you must make sure that the form arrives by the deadline date given, as failure to do so almost automatically rules out your application. You also need to include the job number on the form, if appropriate.

Increasingly, application forms can be filled in online. This has the advantage of giving you direct access to a pre-developed form; although (as with emails) it is very easy to send something that contains errors, so check the form thoroughly before you press 'send'. You will usually get an email confirmation that your form has been received. A useful tip for the longer sections on the form is to complete them in a word processing package first and then copy and paste them onto the form, enabling you to use a spell-checker and other tools.

Always keep a copy of the form, and any research you did on the organization and job area. If you get an interview you will need to revisit all this information.

References

Application forms will ask for two and sometimes more references, usually from a previous employer or tutor. Your university tutors, those who know you best, are the most useful people to approach. Email is probably the best way to ask. Remind them who you are and remember that they do not have to give a reference, so be polite rather than demanding.

If they agree, they will ask for information about the job. Send them all you can, including the person specification. The time frames on references are often very short, so all the information you can give will be welcome.

The person specification revisited

Most application forms end with a blank sheet inviting you to give further information about yourself in support of your application. This is a very important part of the form as you can use it in relation to the essential and desirable criteria in the person specification. Go through all of the criteria and reflect on your experiences, qualifications and the content of your course, matching what you have done against them.

You need to draw parallels between what the criteria state and what you have done. For example, one of the criteria might be 'experience of working in partnership with a variety of sectors and agencies'. You may not think that you have done this, but your university experience may well be relevant. For instance, the following shows how one student used her experiences at university to show how she could fulfil the criteria.

I understand the importance of working in partnership with a variety of different sectors and agencies. In order to do this I have made it my business to find out as much as I possibly can about the work of all the schools in the area and the various agencies that you work with such as educational psychologists, education welfare officers (EWOs), behaviour support teams, health and social services. I have carried out interviews about the challenges of partnership working with teachers and social workers and completed a special assignment on factors that make for effective partnerships in local authority settings.

Another of the essential criteria might include, 'the ability to work well under pressure and to tight deadlines'. One student responded, and was successful, with the following:

Over the past three years I have successfully completed a whole range of assignments on time and to a very good standard. This has been while also holding down two part-time jobs and maintaining a long-term commitment to a local voluntary agency where I offer childcare support. This voluntary work means that I am frequently telephoned at very short notice to offer respite childcare for families in difficulty. If this happens than I have to rapidly re-schedule my other commitments in order to fulfil these responsibilities as well.

In addition, employers often ask for skills in project management. This involves planning, monitoring and evaluating the work that you are undertaking. Your entire university career will have involved this sort of activity, including working with others in order to develop a project related to an assignment. Here is how one student drew on her experience in response to this criterion.

As part of my course I have frequently needed to work with others to plan out and deliver various projects. This has involved assigning tasks, setting deadlines, meeting and reviewing progress, producing the finished article whether this be a presentation or some other kind of project, receiving feedback and using this to carry out reflection and evaluation for future work.

You should always give examples of things that you have actually done to show that you meet the criteria. A student responding to the criterion 'ability to establish good working relationships with all service providers' in the following way would probably not be shortlisted as the comments are too vague and woolly.

I think it is very important to develop good working relationships and I have always tried to do so. Good working relationships mean a lot to me and I like to think that I am a good colleague.

The comment offers potential employers no way of knowing whether the student has done anything that would show that they can put these desires into practice.

Similarly, the following response to the criterion 'excellent interpersonal and communication skills' is also problematic.

My comunication skills are great! Everybody says so! Im a good talker and an even better listener.

This student has made no reference to any other kinds of communication other than speaking and listening. While these are vital, the ability to communicate in writing, by email, in reports, through presentations and so on is similarly important.

In addition, the student does not demonstrate the ability to use different sorts of registers – ways of addressing an audience – for different circumstances. The approach above is far too informal for a letter of application.

Finally, the basic spelling mistakes and typos suggest to a potential employer that there is a big gap between this person's perception of themselves and their actual ability when it comes to interpersonal and communication skills.

The job specification

The job specification lists a series of duties and responsibilities associated with the post. The specification in Figure 5.2 is a typical example, and the following discussion focuses on how you might go about applying for this post, and how your degree might be used to provide evidence that you are the person for the job.

Again, when you see one of these documents it is important to consider the criteria in relation to the knowledge, skills and values that you have gained at university. If you were to apply for this post, you would need to go through each of the units or modules that you have covered on your course and list the relevant knowledge that you have gained.

Knowledge

You could, for instance, think about what you know about the organization, asking yourself whether you know what Sure Start is, how it evolved and how it is funded.

You might find it useful to consider what you know about how it relates to other providers and organizations. For instance, have you knowledge about Early Years Developments in Childcare Partnerships? Do you know about any other agencies that Sure Start works with?

There is also the wider, political context. Ask yourself what you know about the development of childcare, the legislation involved and the various issues related to looking for good quality childcare. What have you learnt about the way in which government policy has responded to the childcare challenge, and how has it been linked to other agendas, such as regeneration and anti-poverty? What knowledge have you gained about

Community Engagement Worker: Sure Start £19,770–22,971

- The post requires energy and enthusiasm to enable families of under 4s in the Sure Start area to access better childcare, health care and education.

- To work with parents, carers and community representatives to enable the identification of local needs and to develop services that respond to those needs.

- To devise strategies and approaches to ensure the involvement of hard to reach families and children in the catchment area.

Duties and responsibilities

- To work to the Sure Start ethos to implement a community engagement strategy, which ensures the process of ongoing community participation in the Sure Start Region X Programme.

- To ensure the involvement of hard to reach families in the Sure Start catchment area.

- Liaise with families, other key workers and relevant organizations.

- Help to develop support groups and family support networks.

- To monitor achievement against Sure Start targets and outcomes.

- To provide broad-based advice and guidance to families of under 4s.

- To link local, regional and national initiatives in a strategic way.

- To research, develop and prepare funding applications.

- To produce reports as required under the terms and conditions of the programme.

- To support and assist in the development of childcare facilities and services.

- Work as part of a Sure Start integrated team.

- Any other duties as may be required by the Programme Manager.

Figure 5.2 A typical job specification

the challenges inherent in this agenda: lack of time, resources, issues around access and so on?

Other relevant knowledge will be about children and families. Ask yourself what you know about development needs and the different perspectives about children's needs. Consider how you have begun to explore and analyse the various perspectives of professionals, parents and children themselves, as that will help you to tune in to different stakeholders' perceptions of what is in the best interests of children. What debates have you been introduced to in relation to families with particular difficulties or access issues or special educational needs?

In addition, there are aspects of how you gained this knowledge about Sure Start that might be useful to think through when applying for this job. For instance, a key question is *how* you know what you know. Has it been through talking and listening to key stakeholders, through reading and research, through observation, or any other methods?

There are also issues about professional practice here. For instance, what has your course taught you about the challenges and tensions embedded in multi-disciplinary working? What has it taught you about different professional perspectives and the challenges of enabling people to work outside of their particular professional boxes? What have you learnt about professional cultures and the power of different professions and the role of professions and professionals within society? Have you been exposed to different environments where professionals work and has this helped you to gain an understanding of different cultures and contexts?

Finally, you could think through which assignments you have done that have helped you to unpack these issues and whether your course has introduced you to ethical issues relating to collecting information and presenting it in different formats.

Skills

The next stage is to consider what relevant skills you have. For instance, your degree will have honed your ability to consider different perspectives on issues and attitudes. Here you can draw on assignments where you did well or where you tackled a relevant topic area for this particular post. This could include assignments where you interviewed someone with a responsibility for children's care or education, such as professionals working in the community.

Collating and organizing information gathered either from books, journals or from talking to relevant individuals and producing essays and reports as a result will have given you skills in both writing and researching. These skills can also be used to gather information that can help you prepare funding applications. Even if you have never prepared one of these you have learnt how to use the Web, how to sort out authoritative sources from those that cannot be trusted and how to carry out investigations to narrow down fields of enquiry to a really focused end.

You may also have had to produce a draft or a proposal for your dissertation, if you had to do one. In doing so you will have convinced your tutors that you had a good understanding of the scope of the project and of the resources needed. This is very like a research bid. Further, this can be seen to demonstrate time management and project management skills. These will also have been demonstrated through your completion of other assignments where you planned and managed your own learning.

Finally, you will have developed your collaborative skills, for example by undertaking group presentations or negotiating access to settings or individuals.

Values and beliefs

Any employer will look at an application form hoping to find some assurance that you have values and beliefs that mean that you will fit into their team.

In relation to this, your course will have given you opportunities to examine your beliefs about children and children's needs, making you very self-aware. In addition, you will have learnt to argue your case and present your reasons for your beliefs or actions clearly.

You will also be able to recognize the way that people's attitudes are related to their professional training, personal experiences, upbringing and culture. Alongside this will be an awareness of the need to be non-judgemental and tolerant of other people's opinions.

Further, you will have had to address issues around equality of opportunity and children's rights and those who are often seen as underrepresented such as those with special educational needs or from minority ethnic groups.

In responding to the job description, then, you will need to show that you have an awareness of the challenges inherent in representing a range of different views and ideas.

In summary

Knowledge: stress the fact that you are up to date with recent and relevant information around legislation, child development, topical issues, social care, education issues and children's rights.

Skills: stress the fact you have learnt to research, study, analyse, problem solve, communicate, organize, discuss, prioritize, listen and debate.

Values and beliefs: stress the fact that you are flexible, child centred, open, tolerant, have an awareness of different opinions and a commitment to equal opportunities.

INTERVIEWS

If you have been shortlisted you will receive a letter giving you the time and date of your interview along with a map, details of how to get to the venue and a contact number for you to confirm you are going to attend. It is very important that you confirm your attendance. You would be amazed by how many people fail to do this.

Getting to an interview means that you have shown the staff doing the shortlisting that you fulfil the criteria on the job specification and the person specification, at least enough for them to want to meet you face to face.

You now need to think about how you are going to perform well. To begin with, get out the copy of the application form that you made, to remind yourself of what you said. Gather together all the material you can about the organization – something that will be fairly easy, as you will have done some research before you first asked for the information about the job. You will also find that leaflets like 'Preparing for Interviews', available from the careers service, give checklists that will help you.

Getting there in time

You should be at the venue at least 15 minutes before you are actually due. Make sure that you know exactly where the interview is to take place and if at all possible do a dry run so that you know the public transport routes, or, if you are going by car, where you can park. There is nothing worse than arriving for an interview thinking you have plenty of time and then finding yourself unable to park or, having found a space, not having appropriate change for a machine.

What to wear

First impressions *are* important. Think about the job you are applying for and who is going to be interviewing you.

If this is a job that is office based, wear something that you could conceivably wear to work and make sure that it is smart, clean and presentable. Similarly, if the job you are applying for means you will work directly with children, you need to think carefully about the kinds of clothes that you wear, for instance to show that you look comfortable and appropriate around young children.

Presentations

Candidates are now frequently asked to prepare a short presentation to deliver before interview. If this is the case, the letter offering you an interview will give you a title which you are to present upon. You will also be told how long the presentation is to last and whether there is any technology available that you can use. If PowerPoint or overhead projectors (OHPs) are available then you need to decide if you *want* to use them (as the other candidates may), and be sure that you know *how* to use them.

Your presentation should be rehearsed in front of a mirror and to an audience. This will allow you to practise giving appropriate eye contact and hopefully help you get over any fears you may have. As you have given presentations as part of your degree, however, you have had practice at this before, and that should give you confidence.

Some of the basic requirements of a presentation are that you should:

- Keep to time. If for any reason you do run out of time, take a breath, summarize in a sentence and finish. You will lose marks for your presentation if you substantially over-run or under-run.

- Ensure all of your slides or overheads are clearly visible and contain only the essential information.

- Have notes that you are comfortable with handling (small cards tied together work well).

- Make sure you look at your audience, smile and pace yourself so that your words are not garbled.

- Position yourself so that you are not blocking anybody's view of the slides (if you decide to use them) and ensure that you do not have your back to any member of the audience.

Remember that everybody is nervous in interview so the panel expect some hesitation and nervousness and will try to put you at ease.

The interview questions

Most interviews consist of a series of questions that are delivered by each member of the interview panel, usually in turn. There should be the same initial questions to each candidate. While you are answering these questions it is quite common for the interviewers to be scribbling comments. This can be off-putting, but is necessary to enable them to judge who is the best candidate. You need to concentrate solely on what you want to say.

Usually, interviews will include a variation on the theme of 'why do think we should give you this job?' Even if this question is not asked directly it is really important to have rehearsed in your own mind why you should be appointed to the post, by thinking through what skills and knowledge you can bring to it.

Attitude

Interviews are a kind of performance. To engage the audience, the interviewers, and give yourself a chance of getting the post, you need to come across as an enthusiastic, committed and positive potential member of staff.

From the point of view of the employer, it costs a lot of money to recruit staff. Apart from the cost of the adverts and mailings there is also the time involved in the recruitment process, the interviewing itself, the administration of all of the forms and the follow-up discussions. In addition, once the person is in post they may need further training. See the interview as your opportunity to convince those listening to you that it will be time and money well spent.

Questions from you

At the end of the interview you will be asked if you have any questions for the panel. It is always good to have one or two questions in hand, but you need to think about the impression that the questions you choose to ask give of you. For example, a question like *'do you think I'd have any chance of getting a holiday after I've worked here for 6 months?'* could give the impression that you are not actually very committed.

In contrast, asking a question that enhances something that you have been told already shows your willingness to develop and grow into the job. A good question, for example, could be, *'are there opportunities for further development and a chance to take on new initiatives?'* Alternatively, *'could you give me some idea of the kind of induction that you would be offering for the post to the successful candidate?'* gives an impression of commitment.

If you genuinely do not have a question then say so, but word it carefully. Something like *'everybody's been so helpful today that all my questions have been answered'* suggests that you have valued and appreciated the information that you have been given, while a simple 'no' actually sounds rather too blunt, even if it is true.

Finally, before you leave the room thank everybody for giving you their time, shake hands if the interview was sufficiently formal for this and remember to collect your coat and bag.

Feedback

If everything has gone well then you get the best feedback of all – hearing that you have got the job. However, given the competitive nature of the job market, it may be that you miss out. It is always sensible, once you have got over the disappointment, to ask for feedback on your performance. Almost any organization will be happy to give you feedback and you need to take it in the spirit in which it is intended, namely that it should be seen as a way of helping you to do better next time.

Specifically seek feedback on what went well but also on how you could improve an application in the future. It is likely that your letter of application was strong and that is why you got through to the interview, but it may be that you needed more experience or that some of your answers indicated that you needed more knowledge about some aspects of the role.

Write down the feedback that you get and think about it seriously. Plan two or three things that you can do as a result of the feedback and give yourself a time frame as to when you are going to do them. Share the feedback with people that you trust who are in a position to help you to achieve some of the things that the feedback has suggested.

The feedback may suggest that you had appropriate knowledge and skills but that your values or attitudes did not fit in with that of the organization concerned. The interview process allows those interviewing to gauge whether they think somebody would fit into the culture of an organization and be happy in it. However, just because you do not fit in one organization does not mean that you will not fit in with another, so persist. You will find a job where you can use the skills you have gained.

Chapter 6

Life Afterwards

This chapter is designed to help you benefit from the experiences of people who have finished CS/ECS degrees and have moved into the world of graduate employment. It is based on conversations with former students about the jobs and courses they are doing now and how their university studies are helping them to be successful. By listening to their stories you will pick up some useful ideas about:

- the sort of career options that are available to you

- what such work entails

- the sorts of knowledge, skills and qualities their work involves.

The graduates you will hear from in this chapter will talk about things they did that helped them get ahead of the competition for jobs, or things they wish they'd done when they were undergraduates. Hearing such advice straight from the horse's mouth will help you see the sorts of things that you can do while you are still at university to improve your chances of finding and getting future employment you will enjoy.

Our graduates' stories will also show you the wide variety of ways in which you can use CS/ECS courses in your own life after university. It will highlight how you are unlikely simply to build up specific professional skills geared to working directly with children (as you would on a vocational course) but can use your course and your time at university to

- develop new interests and widen your horizons

- build up a personal profile of expertise

- adapt the course to suit your own individual needs and interests

- gain relevant experience and knowledge

- develop key skills, including critical thinking, which will stand you in good stead to apply for and pursue further professional qualifications.

WHERE ARE THEY NOW?

Following graduation CS/ECS students go into a diverse range of roles, and not all of them work with, or even for, children or young people. However, a good number do go on to teach in primary schools, or to manage or co-ordinate services or projects for children or adolescents, or to work with parents and families, or are employed in multi-professional children's services, and a few go on to do childhood-related research. Find out what sort of jobs people from your course have gone into, as it may prompt you to think about new possibilities.

Examples of the varied future career paths our own students have taken include:

- Children's Fund Participation Officer

- Children's Rights Officer

- Inclusion worker

- Early Years Development and Childcare Partnership development officer

- Parent Participation worker employed by voluntary sector providers

- Sure Start Childcare providers

- Speech and language therapy support worker

- Asylum seekers/homeless families officer

- Family Learning Co-ordinator within a Local Education Authority

- Education Liaison Officer working at the interface between schools/colleges and universities

- Nursery Manager

- Learning Mentor (special needs)

- Manager of children's respite services

- Postgraduate Certificate in Education (PGCE)

- Diploma in Social Work

- Children's publishing

- OFSTED Registered Inspector

- Senior Research Assistant working in an university research unit

- MA/MSc degrees in Social Research, Social Policy, Childhood Studies, Psychology, Women's Studies

- Human Resource Management.

Case studies of CS/ECS students' first destinations following their degree

In the boxes below you can read about some of the opportunities taken up by CS/ECS students immediately after they finished their courses. In each, we give you a feel for the work, an idea of what it entails, and their views on why and how they chose to follow that particular route.

CASE STUDY

Education Liaison Officer

On leaving university Heather went to work for another university's student recruitment office. Her job mainly involved delivering talks to Year 12 students in local colleges and schools and was targeted at young people whose socio-economic backgrounds meant that they were unlikely to think about attending university. Heather's job was to

- raise awareness about the benefits of higher education

- help youngsters see what student life was really like

- generally raise the aspirations and confidence of young people in the region

- encourage them to consider applying to university.

CONTINUED

The initiative that funded her post also put on a range of activity days and residential visits designed to offer a taste of student life. These included

- running subject taster sessions
- study skills activities
- facilitating the shadowing of current university students
- allowing young people the chance to participate in summer schools that enabled them to demonstrate their potential to be a successful university student.

Although Heather initially started her CS course thinking that she would like to work with younger children, during the degree she found she actually enjoyed working with older children and young adults, although this was something she hadn't considered at all before coming to university. In her comments about this job she places a lot of emphasis on reflecting on people's values, children's voices and the critical thinking skills she has developed as part of her degree, which she now draws upon in her professional role:

I am working with schools and colleges from Excellence in Cities areas, who by nature do not have special advantages that many people take for granted. Childhood Studies did open my eyes to the diversity of children's experiences and educational circumstances and made me think about my reaction towards them. Working with children as research participants during the Childhood Studies degree made me think critically about how the project's aims could be achieved. I helped to develop feedback from the youngsters taking part in the project, and especially built on the research methods we'd explored that try to overcome the power imbalance in the adult–child relationship, so young people could have a say.

CASE STUDY

Going into teaching

On leaving university Carolyn secured a place on a PGCE. She had always known that she wanted to teach and built up a bank of knowledge to support that aim throughout her university career, particularly as she wanted English as her subject specialism. Here she talks about how she ensured that she took units during her course that enabled her to fulfil her aim. Her comments emphasize that this is important to bear in mind on a general CS/ECS degree.

I always wanted to be a primary school teacher: I knew that from the beginning of the course. Others competing with you to get on a PGCE have subject knowledge, having done a more traditional degree, like Maths, or English. I felt quite daunted by that at first. So I sought advice from my Guidance Tutor, early on, and was told to broaden my knowledge base.

Then, when I was taking Childhood Studies I was very conscious that I'd need to build up a sound subject base for my teaching career. So I did what my Guidance Tutor said: I took stock of the subjects I felt good at, like English and German, and decided I had quite strong linguistic skills. So I worked towards choosing English as my subject specialism as I went through the course, to boost that up. For example, I chose a unit on picture books and one on geography in my second year option, to give me National Curriculum subject knowledge.

CASE STUDY

Human Resource Manager

Elaine decided that she didn't want to work with or for children, but was interested instead in working with and supporting other people more generally. She decided, therefore, she would like to work in human resources. Immediately after graduation she applied for a hugely competitive National Health Service Graduate Training scheme, for which there were only 12 places nationally. She came extremely close to getting accepted, and here talks about how she felt about the experience and having set her sights so high:

CONTINUED

Unfortunately I was not successful in gaining a place on the scheme, but I am pleased I went through the experience, as I now know what to expect if I apply to any others. It was not a waste of time as I have also been contacted recently by a member of management from the graduate schemes asking if I would like them to circulate my CV around NHS organizations in the area, explaining to the employers that I was very close to getting on the scheme. So I may still get a job out of it.

Elaine soon secured work in her chosen area, having proven her worth in a part-time job she'd held during the course of her university studies:

Having finished my degree I returned to work at my local supermarket where I had already been for five years. Not long after graduating, I was shown an internal advert for the post of 'in-store trainer'. My deputy manager suggested I apply and all I had to do was send a letter and a copy of my CV. The post I have now is temporary but it has given me that first step on the ladder and provided me with that much-needed experience of working in a human resources/training environment that will hopefully enable me to progress with my career in this area.

CASE STUDY

Research Assistant

Sarah wasn't entirely sure what she wanted to do when she left university although she had always enjoyed and been good at academic study. She considered going into postgraduate study, but at this stage, funding a higher degree proved to be quite a challenge.

I left uni with very little idea of where I wanted to be; I really wanted to go on to further studies but couldn't afford it and, looking back, I'm glad I didn't go straight into a higher degree as I have come to appreciate how much I am able to learn in employment. I was very lucky getting my first job in research; my dissertation supervisor at uni contacted me, asking if I was interested in doing some research for a Midlands university (I had no prior paid research experience), evaluating a pre-school programme for literacy. My dissertation had focused on a similar subject,

CONTINUED

looking at a pre-school initiative encouraging parents to share books with babies – this is why my dissertation supervisor thought I might be interested. I'm very, very grateful to her for suggesting I apply for this research position – this post confirmed for me research was a career I would like to pursue.

After this short-term research position, I became a Research Assistant at the Sustainable Cities Research Institute. I was initially employed to evaluate two Sure Start programmes. My employer was keen for me to develop my understanding across various disciplines within Sustainable Cities, assigning me to a variety of projects, including: a credit union feasibility study, a handyperson scheme feasibility study, local authority health theme evaluation, a local inquiry into citizen participation, an evaluation of a crèche training course, and an Identification, Referral and Tracking (IRT) pilot evaluation. As well as gaining an understanding of a range of subject areas, this has enabled me to work alongside a number of researchers of different levels, each with a particular style and range of skills, which has been of great benefit to me.

My day-to-day activities are varied – it depends which project I'm working on at the time and the stage I am at with it. I can be working on three different projects so could be involved in the proposal stage, project design, literature search and review, data collection, progress reports/feedback meetings, analysis, report writing, presentations.

CASE STUDY

Inclusion Worker

When Sue left university she wanted to work to support families with young children with special needs. When she successfully applied for the post of Inclusion Worker, her work placed her in a team of officers who work closely with the voluntary sector.

Her day-to-day work involves working with and in playgroups where there are young children who need one-to-one support in order to access the activities alongside other children. She also works with other

CONTINUED

professionals, such as speech therapists, physiotherapists and educational psychologists to assess children's needs, thus ensuring that their move to school or nursery is successful.

I was always very committed to inclusive practice for children with special educational needs. Playgroups are the first place that a parent with a child with SEN leaves that child in the care of 'stranger', and that's a big step for everyone in the family to take. So my role involves me getting to know the child and building up the confidence of the parents, so that they feel reassured that their child will be safe in the new setting.

MOVING INTO EMPLOYMENT

Ensure that potential employers understand your degree

Competition in graduate employment and for further study is fierce and so CS/ECS graduates need to market their qualities carefully and explicitly. Be prepared to explain and justify your CS/ECS course when you leave university as not all employers have a sound grasp of what these courses actually might entail. When faced with a comment like 'Good grief, so you've got a degree in baby-sitting!' it's as well to have thought through how you can highlight the rigours and particular slant of your degree. It is likely, for example, that your ECS degree has equipped you with up-to-date knowledge of recent initiatives and approaches in the early years sector, so be sure to spell these out and highlight, say, your knowledge of Sure Start, family support, multi-agency working, Every Child Matters, and so on. Alternatively, if you are a CS graduate applying for a Children's Rights Officer role, make sure you outline the ways in which you have gained knowledge and insight into children's rights policy, legislation and issues as part of your degree.

Employers may also have misperceptions of CS/ECS degrees if they are accustomed to recruiting or working with students from more vocational child-related fields. It's not uncommon for, say, head teachers, to assume that CS/ECS degrees are competency- or skills-based vocational courses.

Many students actually get a first taste of these misperceptions if their course offers research observation visits to nurseries or schools. You may have found that teachers and nursery officers saw you as a student teacher on placement and so you may well be already skilled in explaining how your course differs from more 'hands-on' degrees. If not, you should think about how you will address these misconceptions when you are applying for jobs, and even when you go to visit your Careers Service.

BE SURE TO MARKET YOUR COURSE-RELATED KNOWLEDGE AND SKILLS EFFECTIVELY

Because courses vary so much, and because of what we outline above, you need to think about the ways in which your CS/ECS degree is valuable and relevant for the career you wish to pursue.

Successful students often choose to draw employers' attention to the nature and value of the independent research skills that have been developed on their degrees. Keep a learning log to note down key elements. For example, if you are going into higher degree work, or contract-research, you will want to illuminate what you know and have learned about the research process. The following graduate, now working as a research assistant, looks back and reflects upon the way in which she could perhaps have sold her skills and qualities more forcefully and confidently, had she realized them at the time she applied for research posts.

I'm now involved in the whole research process, from producing proposals to disseminating research findings, I contribute to each aspect. This has been a gradual process: moving from data collection to analysis, then report writing and presentation of findings, and most recently to include preparing proposals.

My degree prepared me for this position more than I realized. Only when I look back can I see that I learned the basics of carrying out a research project (from design to data collection, analysis and writing up). When I consider my role today, I see that the elements of my dissertation research project are present in all the projects I'm currently involved with.

Strategically use opportunities to undertake research or independent project work in CS/ECS

Even if you don't plan to go into a research post or higher degree after university, CS/ECS graduates will advise you to think hard about, say, selecting your dissertation topic area, so that you build up and can evidence the knowledge, experience and expertise you might need when it comes to looking for work. Successful graduates choose something that will give them a head start at an interview, and may influence their own practice in future. Here, for example, is the student you heard from earlier, who wanted to go into teaching and to build up her knowledge of the English curriculum.

I decided to do my dissertation linked to English. I wanted to gain knowledge of the literacy hour, but I focused in on an aspect – shared reading – that interested me. I interviewed experienced and newly qualified teachers about how and why they used shared reading. I really got to grips with the different values and attitudes of the staff involved. I learned there was so much going on, and there are lots of approaches that have a big impact on how children learn. It gave me the chance to learn from experienced teachers: I'll certainly be including story-time for a purpose, now, because I can see how important it is. I suppose I'm much more aware of the value of reading and the importance that you have to place on it.

And here is another, who was interested in inclusion of young children with special needs.

I knew I wanted to support childminders working with SEN children, so I did my dissertation on childminders' perceptions of quality. I compared that with OFSTED's definitions of quality. Doing this made me clearer about what makes a quality setting, so I was confident about putting forward my views about why certain practices were good and what was important to children's development when I went for my job interview.

I guess I'd already rehearsed my ideas, thought a lot about why I believed certain things, and was used to explaining the reasons for my views. They asked me about how I thought a setting should keep a child safe, and I saw it in a more complicated way than I would otherwise have done before I did my dissertation. Instead of just talking about putting child-proof locks on doors and

*fitting stair gates, I talked about how building effective relationships with chil-
dren, where they are treated, within reason, as being able to talk about and
understand what is dangerous and what keeps them safe, can have a significant
impact on keeping children safe.*

In both cases their dissertation choices built up subject specific knowledge, but also allowed them to use their research to talk in considerable
depth with relevant professionals, learning from their experience and
gaining a genuine insight into their chosen careers. These students also
used their research to reflect on and establish their own values, philosophical stance and approach to working with children. The degree
allowed them the luxury of time and space to engage in such reflection
before they were forced to make decisions in the challenging environment of the workplace, encumbered by professional responsibilities and
obligations. Unsurprisingly, the first student went on to become, in the
view of one of her PGCE tutors, 'an excellent teacher'.

Here is another example of using research to develop future professional
capital. This ECS student became fascinated with issues of inclusion and
entitlement with regard to young children with special educational needs
during her degree. She, too, talks about using the dissertation to help her
get to where she wanted to be.

*I was actually amazed at how relevant my Early Childhood degree was once I
started going for jobs. It turned out to be so up to date about recent approaches,
which have been subject to a lot of fast-paced change, that people [in the field]
were saying to me 'You're so lucky to have had the chance to spend three years
studying all these things, when we have been struggling to keep abreast of it all
by reading the newspapers'. So it wasn't just a case of having stuff to say and
feeling confident talking about Sure Start, the Children Act, Every Child
Matters, Children's Centres, multi-agency working, family support links with
early years and so on – it was that it suddenly hit home quite how much I had
to offer! That felt amazing!*

*When I thought about it, I'd actually written essays on all sorts of issues that
have a massive impact on the world of work in early years – I'd looked at different views of quality, I'd carried out interviews with key professionals and parents, I'd visited a range of different settings – family centres, children's centres,
Sure Start, local programmes, Early Excellence Centres, and we'd had visitors*

in from all of them who'd come to talk with us and share their experiences and ideas. I'd heard practitioners talk about the tensions and challenges they face in their work, how they're trying to get to grips with some of the problems managers face when they want to bring about change, and suddenly it drove home how relevant it all was. I mean, I know exactly how to look up information, I know the websites and that to be able to update my knowledge, for one thing. But it's more than that, really. In fact, I wish I'd been a bit more sensible and thought about this sooner, because then I'd have been more focused and made more of the opportunities on my course – made more of the essays and so on – if only I had seen the point sooner, instead of just doing assignments because I had to, just to get a mark to pass. That was, with hindsight, a bit of a waste, really – I could've made much more of it.

Highlight your generic key skills

Remember that employers will see your degree in line with any other, because it represents graduate standards in key areas, such as communication, critical thinking, project management and so on. On a CS/ECS degree the third year will typically allow you to demonstrate that you can manage your own time, make decisions, not rely exclusively upon someone else to tell you what to do, that you know how to find out about things – in fact, all the skills and qualities of independence and decision-making that employers often look for in their graduates.

Another worry I had was that my degree was not specific enough for the type of work I wanted. Again, I discussed this with the careers adviser and also my tutors and decided to focus all my work, especially my dissertation, on topics that related to my chosen career. The way this degree is structured allows you quite a bit of freedom to tailor it to your own needs. I was also reassured my degree would not be a problem when I started job-hunting and found that a surprising number of employers did not require specific degrees, it was more usual for them to want a 2:1 or a 2:2, or simply a 'good degree', in any subject.

You need, however, to be sure to take every opportunity to consciously develop and enhance these skills both within and outside your degree programme, as they will really count when it comes to life after university.

Degree work helped me to develop generic skills in areas such as time manage-ment, presentation skills and critical thinking. Through working with others in seminars and from practical work in schools I also developed the social skills necessary to help me find a job once I'd graduated.

During my degree I became far more confident of my ability in stressful situa-tions (completing assignments to deadline, doing presentations with fellow undergraduates, undertaking data collection through interview for my disserta-tion). You'll need confidence and flexibility in work. My work involves inter-viewing professionals, and you definitely need to be confident in your approach, especially if you're young and female – you have to get used to patronising tones and don't let them affect you!

Make sure you develop and market appropriate course-related skills

The skills you develop on your CS/ECS course may be specifically related to certain types of future employment. For example, this graduate, who secured a job as an advocate for young people, drew upon the children's rights element of her course to highlight her suitability for the post. She also drew upon what she calls the 'people skills' she developed as part of her course, such as working with others, developing the confidence to express her views and persuade other people, and presentation skills (which can also be marketed as generic skills). She sees this as a matter of trying to understand and respect other people's perspectives, values and attitudes. This now underpins the way she carries out her work and informs how she approaches and deals with young people. In other words, she has learnt to articulate and explain the value of her particular CS course, and the importance of the values, attitudes and approaches that were fostered within it.

I have gained a great deal from the course that is relevant for working with any kind of people. I find myself thinking about the ways in which we work with people, and questioning presumptions made about their lives. Rather than making decisions on their behalf, I am keen to give the participants the lead in making choices about their futures through feedback and discussion groups, as well as simply providing an environment in which they feel able to express their views.

You can also highlight your child-centred values, as this teacher does:

Above all, though, CS helped me to understand why children may behave or react in the ways that they do, and I know I treat them with respect as individuals.

Or as this PGCE student does:

I think I'll be a better teacher having done Childhood Studies because I understand children as people, and see the whole child. I think I'm more likely to make an effort to listen and take children seriously, although I know there'll be pressures that will mean that's quite difficult to achieve. But at least forewarned is forearmed. I feel I've got a broader picture about the education system and children's roles within it to hang onto, especially when I'm starting out.

⬤ Reflecting on your course and relating it to the relevant sector

Make sure you take stock of the relevance of the subjects you are studying and think positive! Again, a learning log might be useful.

I felt quite daunted going for my PGCE interview, because I don't have a normal subject degree. But when I thought about it, I realized that I'd got other skills and knowledge to offer. I had a lot of knowledge about children and how they learn. I knew more than anyone else going for interview about child development, for example. I know an awful lot about how and when children generally learn to achieve things, so I think that'll help me be realistic in my expectations of children, and I talked about how that would help me in a teacher's role.

I'd also done a lot of units that were directly relevant to teaching, and gave me a broader view of education and school. Schooling in Childhood gave me a broad overview of the National Curriculum, special needs, the history of how schools came to be as they are, how they are run, school governors, about OFSTED, LEAs, general policy and practice overview – all sorts of useful things like that. I found having that broad overview was important at the interview, knowing about the issues.

We also did a unit on children's learning on Childhood Studies. I learned about different teaching approaches, and learning styles. I looked particularly at assessment, which is a massive issue in schools now. I became interested in children's self-evaluation skills, and consulting with children is very much being promoted now. For my coursework activities, which built up to that assignment, I interviewed a teacher about the ways she uses annotated work in English, Maths and Science. It was all about giving the child a voice, and to help them think about their learning. That gave me ideas for strategies I might use when I become a teacher, and I learned that children can make decisions, if they're asked. Before I wouldn't have thought like that. I'd have thought teachers should do that for them. So I guess the course just made me think, be a bit more open to trying out ideas for getting children involved in learning, which is a big issue nowadays: how to involve children.

KEEP FOCUSED ON YOUR COURSE'S KEY ISSUES

These graduates return time and again to the *issues* that their course made them engage with. On CS/ECS degrees these are likely to be topical and relevant, so will come into their own in your life after university. For that reason, it's a good idea to make the most of assignments in which you are asked to discuss and explore them. The sooner you see their relevance, the sooner your studies all fall into place, helping you to make the most of your time at university – even modules that don't seem directly connected to your chosen career may well have this sort of relevance.

When I went for my interview I had lots to say. They asked me, for instance, to tell them about an episode in which I had taught a child in school, and how I approached that. They wanted to know what I knew about how children learn, how I would structure activities, how I would respond to them, and help them progress. As well as having direct experience from what I'd done in my own time, I had also thought about these things as part of my course. For example, if I'd have read Granpa to children without having done the 'Picturebooks and developing readers' option unit, I would have just gone through it, reading it as just a story to read at storytime, and that would be it. Now, having looked at how it works, and what kinds of things it's doing, I can see how there are lots of interesting things I can do with it.

That happened as well, when the head teacher on the interview panel asked me to talk about how I'd work with parents. I could talk about a Parents into Schools initiative I'd seen when I was working in school, but I realized I actually knew a lot too, from Perspectives on Parenting, about not being judgemental and making people feel 'bad' parents. So I talked about making them feel welcome in school, and helping them to understand what is being covered in school, and generally working in partnership together. I could easily talk about these things, as they were issues we covered on the course.

USE YOUR UNIVERSITY'S CAREERS SERVICE AND OTHER SUPPORT MECHANISMS

You might feel that it is too early to start thinking about careers, but previous graduates would advise you to begin immediately. Leaving it until the final year may be leaving it too late.

Deciding when to start job-hunting was, perhaps surprisingly, quite a difficult decision. Going through the first two years of university it seems obvious and natural that job-hunting would begin in the third year. However, when I reached the third year I realized this may not be the best option due to the amount of work I had to do for my degree. It soon became apparent that applying for jobs would be very time consuming, and time was something that I did not really have!

Having registered on the relevant websites, I was receiving regular emails informing me of job vacancies and many of these were the type of training schemes I was looking for. There were so many to look through I felt a bit overwhelmed and concerned about my lack of time to job hunt thoroughly. To get some advice on this I made an appointment with the careers adviser at university. I explained everything to her and she agreed that I shouldn't jeopardize my degree by spending too long applying for jobs. She suggested I pick a few key schemes that I would be really keen to get onto and apply for them. If this proved unsuccessful I could then apply to a wider range once I finished my degree. I asked whether she thought my application being for a year after I graduated rather than straight away (most have a September start) would have any effect on the success of the application and she reassured me it shouldn't make any difference. This was a great weight off my mind and I would recommend everyone visit the careers service at least once even if it is just for some reassurance that you are on the right track – job hunting seems straightforward until you set out and suddenly it gets a lot more complicated! It's good to know that there is support available and you are not on your own.

WORKING AS PART OF A TEAM OR ON YOUR OWN

It is always important to think about the nature of the work you will be doing and what your preferences are about working with others. For instance, this graduate talks about some of the implications of working alone as a Research Assistant.

Although the project may have a team of researchers, essentially you're on your own. Out and about a lot, doing interviews all over – so, get used to public transport; as a researcher, you're on it a lot! Also, brush up on map-reading skills – interviews generally take place at participants' workplaces, which could be anywhere!

You can often feel isolated as a researcher – you need to be able motivate yourself, even when working on a project which can be very boring! Also, you need to be aware of your limits and ask for help and support if you need it.

BUILDING UP HANDS-ON EXPERIENCE IN RELEVANT CONTEXTS

Graduates who want to work with children or take postgraduate courses invariably find that they need to build up practical experience outside the course. Again, a learning log could encompass this kind of work as well as academic work, outlining what skills and knowledge you have gained. Voluntary activity can be used to build up this required prior experience during holiday periods and, of course, helps you to decide where you want to head, and what the requirements would be, in time to fit it all in.

In the extract below, for instance, the advice of this graduate to students is to make sure they gain experience of working directly with children and enabling children's learning. The voluntary work also led to other opportunities, as she describes:

At a PGCE interview, obviously you need to show that you can work with and relate to children in school contexts. They want evidence of hands-on experience. That means you have to do quite a lot outside the course.

At first, I went into a school regularly, just helping out – fetching and carrying, and working with children, supporting children in their learning under the direction of the teacher. Because of my interest, the head teacher asked me to take on a specific paid role, supporting children in different classes who needed extra help with their language skills. This was really useful experience; I saw daily school life from the inside, in lots of different classes.

It's worth remembering that you can build up valuable experience via any paid or unpaid employment you take outside your course experience, too.

Sure, my degree provided me with valuable experience of group work, working to deadlines, communication with people at different levels, researching, self-motivation, and presenting. Presentation skills in particular helped me to get my job, as it involves training groups of people and holding full-day inductions – no matter how much I hated doing presentations in first year it has certainly paid off!

But the second area I used to help show my skills was my part-time job in a local supermarket. Although I originally took the job just to earn a bit of extra money, I have always been conscious that what I do there will all go towards enhancing my CV. Therefore I took on jobs such as writing the monthly newsletter for the company.

I would recommend you grab any opportunities to develop your skills at work, no matter how small it may seem, as this is how you are able to sell yourself in an interview. I showed I had practical work experience and working knowledge of the firm itself. This is another tip I would give – take an interest in the company you work for. I was able to discuss the needs of the business simply through things I had learnt during my time working in the store – it may not seem important at the time but it has got me into the job I want.

EARN RESPECT

These stories also show how demonstrating your worth and gaining the respect of those with whom you work, even on an informal basis, can lead to chances you might otherwise not have had. These students had no trouble securing warm recommendations and references from part-time employers, as well as their academic referees, by forging professional working relationships with a range of people throughout and outside their degree programmes. How much better it is to have references from people who genuinely know you and enjoy working with you, than from people who can only report what's on file about you! Forging such relationships, by getting a reputation for acting professionally, enthusiastically and courteously from the outset of your course, has obvious pay-offs for you: the impressions you create as a student and employee are likely to carry over into the references you receive when it comes to life after university.

BE PREPARED FOR ALTERNATIVE SELECTION PROCESSES TO GRADUATE SCHEMES

Some of our graduates apply for jobs whose selection process involves much more than a simple interview and presentation. It's worth finding out about these in advance, so you can be prepared and, of course, only apply if you feel confident of handling such jobs. If you're fazed by the prospect of these selection procedures you probably wouldn't enjoy the demands of the job.

For the first stage I went down to London for a residential. After an interview I had to take part in a group exercise. I think this lasted about 40 minutes and involved six of us reading a scenario and then working through it. We were each given a different role to play and had to act out a meeting in which we were deciding how to prioritize various issues that needed to be looked at within a fictional working situation. We each had our own issue to put forward and of course all were trying to get ours to be the top priority.

It was quite an intense and tiring day but I actually enjoyed much of it. It might sound daft saying try and enjoy the experience but at the end of the day you are either going to get it or you're not and it's not the end of the world if you don't. Being worried and nervous will not help and in fact will probably lessen your chances of being successful as I found out in the final stage.

Having been successful in the interview and group exercise, I was invited to attend a 24-hour assessment at a Conference Centre. This was testing how well you would cope in the role of a manager. We were each given a desk with a lap-top and printer and all the activities were sent via email to the laptop. These included writing reports and attending meetings. The reports were testing how well you could assimilate a lot of information received during a short space of time and in a variety of forms, for example one exercise included a graph show-ing predicted costs of building work, requirements of those who would be using the building, budgets, predicted user numbers, etc. It was then my job to put all this information together into a proposal of what should be done, what the cost would be, and whether or not it could be done with the budget provided.

With only 40 minutes to get through all the information and complete the report I found this extremely difficult. There were also three meetings to attend: one with a colleague, one with a group of colleagues and a representative from another organization, and one with a medical consultant. As with the report, a great deal of information was emailed prior to attending each meeting and this needed to be read, understood and the main points pulled out to be used in the meetings. I found my nerves got the better of me and I panicked due to the vast amount of information I was expected to take in. If I was to go back and do this assessment again I would put in a lot more time preparing for it. I thought I couldn't really prepare as I did not know what to expect; however, speaking to other candidates who had attended other assessments with different organiza-tions I discovered it was quite a common structure. Knowing this, I think I could have made better use of the careers service who do offer help in preparing for this kind of assessment centre.

GOING INTO FURTHER STUDY

There are many reasons why you might choose to do this, from seeing further study as a route to career progression, or because you enjoy the challenges it offers. Talk to others to see what to expect and think through whether it would suit you. The following graduate shares her reasons for her choice to return to study.

I am starting an MSc in Social Research. There are a number of reasons for this – there is little support and training for contract-researchers so any opportunity to progress and develop skills should be snapped up; I want a challenge, I want to get back to learning 'uni style', not just 'on the job' practical learning; and I want to progress up the researcher scale, so need to have a higher degree. I wouldn't recommend going straight from a first degree to a postgrad degree personally – take some time to learn through practice, suss out which postgrad course would be most beneficial to you. Oh – and ask for funding from your employer!

A FINAL WORD

We very much hope that you find our book useful and that you enjoy your course to the full.

We'd like to finish by handing over to one of our most successful students, who looks back over her experience in order to offer what seems extremely important advice:

The main thing I have learnt through all these experiences is to keep a record of everything you do and look upon everything as experience and improving your employability. Some things may seem irrelevant or not important, but you never know when an opportunity may arise that requires you to draw on what you have already done and put those skills into practice. Above all, use the support available – careers service, tutors, websites, and friends. They may have been through similar experiences and can offer advice, or you may ask them to proof-read an application form, or maybe they are just a shoulder to cry on or someone to celebrate with!

Good luck – we wish you every success!

Further reading and resources

The following are useful general texts on the subject of childhood or early childhood, although this list is by no means exhaustive. Nearly all of these authors have written other books which you might also find useful, but many more obviously exist. You'll need, of course, to follow up more specialized reading lists on your own course.

Abbott, L. and Moylett, H. (eds) (1997) *Working with the Under-3s: Training and Professional Development.* Buckingham: Open University Press.

Abbott, L. and Moylett, H. (eds) (1999) *Early Education Transformed.* London: Falmer.

Abbott, L. and Pugh, G. (eds) (1998) *Training to Work in Early Years: Developing the Climbing Frame.* Maidenhead: Open University Press.

Anning, A., Cullen, J. and Fleer, M. (eds) (2004) *Early Childhood Education: Society and Culture.* London: Sage.

Boushel, M., Fawcett, M. and Selwyn, J. (eds) (2000) *Focus on Early Childhood: Principles and Realities.* Oxford: Blackwell Science.

Buckingham, D. (2000) *After the Death of Childhood: Growing Up in the Age of Electronic Media.* Cambridge: Polity.

Corsaro, W. (1997) *The Sociology of Childhood.* London: Sage.

Gittins, D. (1998) *The Child in Question.* Basingstoke: Macmillan.

Goleman, D. (1995) *Emotional Intelligence: Why It Can Matter More Than IQ.* New York: Bantam.

Hill, B., Pike, G. and Selby, D. (1998) *Perspectives on Childhood: An Approach to Citizenship Education.* London: Cassell.

Hill, M. and Tisdall, K. (1997) *Children and Society.* Harlow: Longman.

Holden, C. and Clough, N. (eds) (1998) *Children as Citizens*. London: Jessica Kingsley.

Holland, P. (1992) *What is a Child? Popular Images of Childhood*. London: Virago Press.

Hollindale, P. (1997) *Signs of Childness in Children's Books*. Stroud: Thimble Press.

Holt, J. (1975) *Escape from Childhood: The Needs and Rights of Children*. Harmondsworth: Penguin.

James, A. and Prout, A. (eds) (1997) *Constructing and Reconstructing Childhood: Contemporary Issues in the Sociological Study of Childhood* (2nd Edition). London: Falmer.

James, A., Jenks, C. and Prout, A. (1998) *Theorizing Childhood*. Cambridge: Polity Press.

Jenkins, H. (ed.) (1998) *The Children's Culture Reader*. New York: New York University Press.

Jenks, C. (1992) *The Sociology of Childhood*. Aldershot: Batsford.

Jenks, C. (1996) *Childhood*. London: Routledge.

Jenks, C. (2000) *The Discovery of Childhood*. Hull: CSSC Working Paper No. 2.

Kehily, M. J. (ed.) (2004) *An Introduction to Childhood Studies*. Maidenhead: Open University Press.

Kuhn, A. (1995) *Family Secrets*. London: Verso.

Lee, N. (2001) *Childhood and Society*. Buckingham: Open University Press.

Lesnik-Oberstein, K. (ed.) (1998) *Children in Culture*. Houndmills: Macmillan.

Mayall, B. (ed.) (1994) *Children's Childhoods: Observed and Experienced*. London: Falmer Press.

Mayall, B. (2002) *Towards a Sociology for Childhood: Thinking from Children's Lives*. Buckingham: Open University Press.

Maynard, T. and Thomas, N. (2004) *An Introduction to Early Childhood Studies*. London: Sage.

Mills, J. and Mills, R. (eds) (2000) *Childhood Studies: A Reader in Perspectives of Childhood*. London: Routledge.

Moss, P. and Penn, H. (1996) *Contemporary Issues in Early Childhood*

Education. London: Hodder and Stoughton.

Pilcher, J. and Wagg, S. (eds) (1996) *Thatcher's Children? Politics, Childhood and Society in the 1980s and 1990s.* London: Falmer Press.

Postman, N. (1983) *The Disappearance of Childhood: How TV is Changing Children's Lives.* London: W. H. Allen.

Pugh, G. (ed.) (2001) *Contemporary Issues in the Early Years: Working Collaboratively for Children.* (3rd Edition). London: Sage.

Qvortrup, J., Bardy, M., Sgritta, G. and Wintersberger, H. (eds) (1994) *Childhood Matters: Social Theory, Practice and Politics.* Aldershot: Avebury.

Roberts, R. (2002) *Self-Esteem and Early Learning* (2nd Edition). London: Paul Chapman Publishing.

Rosen, M. (ed.) (1994) *The Penguin Book of Childhood.* Harmondsworth: Penguin.

Scraton, P. (ed.) (1997) *Childhood In Crisis.* London: UCL Press.

Stainton Rogers, R. and Stainton Rogers, W. (1992) *Stories of Childhood: Shifting Agendas of Child Concern.* Hemel Hempstead: Harvester Wheatsheaf.

Taylor, J. and Woods, M. (1998) *Early Childhood Studies: An Holistic Introduction.* London: Arnold.

Warner, M. (1994) *Managing Monsters: Six Myths of Our Time – The 1994 Reith Lectures.* London: Vintage.

Willan, J., Parker-Rees, R. and Savage, J. (eds) (2004) *Early Childhood Studies.* Exeter: Learning Matters.

Wyse, D. (2003) *Childhood Studies: An Introduction.* London: Blackwell.

Wyse, D. and Hawtin, A. (eds) (2000) *Children: A Multi-professional Perspective.* London: Arnold.

Zornado, J. L. (2001) *Inventing the Child: Culture, Ideology, and the Story of Childhood.* New York: Garland.

Further indicative online resources

Again, the following websites are purely designed to give you a start, and we have grouped them under common themes. They are by no means exhaustive and you should follow up specific specialist sites suggested by your own tutors.

EDUCATION/SCHOOLS

Advisory Centre for Education (ACE) www.ace-ed.org.uk/
Basic Skills Agency www.basic-skills-observatory.co.uk/index.php
Department for Education and Skills (DfES) www.dfes.gov.uk/
Education Action Zones www.standards.dfes.gov.uk/eaz/
Literacy Trust www.literacytrust.org.uk/
National Curriculum (online) www.nc.uk.net/home.html
National Literacy Strategy www.standards.dfes.gov.uk/literacy/
National Numeracy Strategy www.standards.dfes.gov.uk/numeracy/
Office for Standards in Education (OFSTED) www.ofsted.gov.uk/
Qualifications and Curriculum Authority (QCA) www.qca.org.uk/

Research

Assessment Reform Group www.assessment-reform-group.org.uk/
Centre for the Social Study of Childhood www.hull.ac.uk/cssc/
Centre for Studies on Inclusive Education www.inclusion.uwe.ac.uk
Effective Provision of Preschool Education Project (EPPE)
www.ioe.ac.uk/cdl/eppe
Joseph Rowntree Foundation Research
www.jrf.org.uk/funding/research/
National Foundation for Educational Research (NFER) www.nfer.ac.uk/
Online journal searching services, e.g.
www.sosig.ac.uk/roads/subject-listing/World-cat/child.html

Voluntary agencies

These vary, some being large charity organizations, including

Barnardos www.barnardos.org.uk/
Childline www.childline.org.uk/
Child Poverty Action Group www.cpag.org.uk
Contact a Family www.cafamily.org.uk
Coram Family www.coram.org.uk/about.htm
Daycare Trust www.daycaretrust.org.uk/
Homestart www.homestart.org.uk/
Joseph Rowntree Foundation www.jrf.org.uk
National Children's Bureau Child Bereavement Network (CBN)
www.ncb.org.uk/cbn/
National Society for the Prevention of Cruelty to Children (NSPCC)
www.nspcc.org.uk
NCH, The Children's Charity www.nch.org.uk/
Save the Children www.savethechildren.org/
The Children's Society www.the-childrens-society.org.uk/

And more specialized charities, some being for specific disability
groups, such as

MENCAP www.mencap.org.uk/
Parents for the Early intervention of Autism (PEACH)
www.peach.org.uk/Home/
SCOPE www.scope.org.uk/action/factsheets/

There are, though, many smaller local voluntary agencies, too numerous
to list.

Family support

Centre for Fun and Families www.funandfamilies.com/
Children's Services Children's National Service Framework
www.dh.gov.uk/PolicyAndGuidance/HealthAndSocialCareTopics/
ChildrenServices/ChildrenServicesInformation/fs/eng/
Families need Fathers www.fnf.org.uk/
Gingerbread www.gingerbread.org.uk/
Parenting Forum www.parenting-forum.org.uk/
Parentline Plus www.parentlineplus.org.uk/templates/home/index.cfm

Young people

A National Voice (for young care leavers) www.anationalvoice.org/
British Youth Council www.byc.org.uk/
Children and Young People's Unit (CYPU) www.cypu.gov.uk/
Student Councils www.studentcouncil.ie/index.htm
Teenage Pregnancy Unit (DfES) www.dfes.gov.uk/teenagepregnancy/

Early years

Birth to Three: a framework to support children in their earliest years
www.surestart.gov.uk/ensuringquality/birthtothreematters/
Bookstart www.bookstart.co.uk/
British Association for Early Education www.early-education.org.uk/
Children's Centres www.surestart.gov.uk/surestartservices/childrenscentres/
DfES www.childcarelink.gov.uk
Early Years Development and Childcare Partnership (EYDCP)
www.surestart.gov.uk/
Four Nations Policy Network www.childpolicy.org.uk
Government education/early years website www.dfes.gov.uk
High Scope www.high-scope.org.uk
National Childminding Association www.ncma.org.uk/
National Day Nursery Association www.ndna.org.uk
Preschool Learning Alliance (playgroups) www.pre-school.org.uk
Surestart www.surestart.gov.uk/

Children's rights

Centre for Europe's Children www.eurochild.gla.ac.uk
Child's Rights Information Network www.crin.org/
Childwatch www.childwatch.uio.no/
Education Otherwise www.education-otherwise.org/
Equal Opportunities Commission www.eoc.org.uk
National Children's Bureau www.ncb.org.uk/ncb/index.asp
National Children's Office www.nco.ie/links/
UK Youth Parliament www.ukyouthparliament.org.uk/
UN Convention on the Rights of the Child www.ohchr.org/english
or www.unhchr.ch/html/menu2/6/crc/treaties/crc.htm
UNICEF www.unicef.org

Libraries and information services

Connexions (Information and advice for young people) www.connexions-direct.com/
Library and Information Services Team (DfES)
www.dfes.gov.uk/library/
Seven Stories: The Centre for Children's Books www.centreforthechildrensbook.org.uk/
Youth Libraries Group (YLG) www.cilip.org.uk/groups/ylg/

Policies and legislation

Children Act www.hmso.gov.uk
Children's Legal Centre www.childrenslegalcentre.com
Child Support Agency: Children First – a new approach to child support www.csa.gov.uk/
Department of Health www.doh.gov.uk/adoption/
Department of Health, National Service Framework for Children
www.dh.gov.uk/
Education Reform Act 1988
www.legislation.hmso.gov.uk/acts/acts1988/Ukpga_19880040_en_1.ht
Every Child Matters www.dfes.gov.uk/everychildmatters
Green paper 1997 *Excellence for All Children: Meeting Special Educational Needs* www.dfes.gov.uk/sengp/
Health and Social Care Act 2001
www.legislation.hmso.gov.uk/acts/acts2001/20010015.htm
Special Educational Needs and Disability Act 2001
www.hmso.gov.uk/acts/acts2001/20010010.htm
Stationery Office www.hmso.gov.uk/acts
The Big Read, National Reading Campaign
www.literacytrust.org.uk/tbr.html
The Children Bill www.publications.parliament.uk/pa/pabills.htm

Child health

Institute of Child Health www.ich.ucl.ac.uk/ich/index.html
National Childbirth Trust (NCT)
www.nctpregnancyandbabycare.com/nct-online/
National Statistics Online, The Health of Children and Young People
www.statistics.gov.uk/children/

Inclusion

Alliance for Inclusive Education www.allfie.org.uk
Centre for Accessible Environments www.cae.org.uk
Children's Play Council www.ncb.org.uk/cpc/
Commission for Racial Equality www.cre.gov.uk
DfES www.dfes.gov.uk/sen
Disability Rights Commission www.drc-gb.org
National Association of SEN www.nasen.org.uk
Social Exclusion Unit www.socialexclusion.gov.uk/

Index